T0323506

"A timely rethinking of the role of agency in leadership. This book provides meaningful, thoughtful advice for every modern leader."
— **Paul Polman** –*Business Leader, Campaigner, and Co-author of Net Positive*

"The timing for this book couldn't be better. This meaningful playbook serves as a guide and call to action for leaders to embrace their personal agency, manage the deep paradoxes of our polarized and chaotic world, lead with purpose and humility, and create sustainable, meaningful value."
— **Angela Cretu** – *Ex-Global CEO, Avon; Board Director; Women Empowerment Advocate; Angel Investor in Female Founders*

"This book is a transformative book that empowers leaders to navigate the complexities of the 21st century with personal agency. In the face of digitalization, environmental challenges, and a polarized world, this book serves as a guiding light and call to action for leaders to proactively shape their own stories and make a meaningful impact in a rapidly changing and increasingly complex world. Highly recommended!"
— **Dr Marc Kahn** – *Chief Strategy and Sustainability Officer, Investec Plc, London*

"In this era of polarization and activism, this book makes a brilliant case for why and how leaders can proactively manage complexity by approaching situations with a mindset of humility, inquiry, and curiosity."
— **Jeanne Meister** – *Best Selling Author and Founder of Future Workplace*

"This book will help leaders find their grip on the rudder, read the winds, and proactively chart a path through the storm to a new and promising future."
— **Sheila Heen** – *Best Selling Author, Founder of Triad Consulting, Professor Harvard Law School*

"The authors really know what they are talking about. Their real-world experience is unparalleled. They unfold how you can learn to "guide the tide" with precision, humility, empathy, and deep knowledge and know-how."
— **Carol Kauffman, PhD** – *Assistant Professor, Harvard Medical School; Founder, Institute of Coaching, Senior Leadership Advisor; Egon Zehnder, Author, Real-Time Leadership*

"The book's lessons are rooted in honesty – skillful honesty with ourselves and others, even when it is challenging; honesty in assessing the truth of our operating context, even when we tend to self-delude; and finally, honesty about what we cannot control but also – and here is the real gift of this book – honesty about what we can and must control, even when it is tempting to abdicate responsibility."
— **Mary Gentile** – *Creator/Director, Giving Voice To Values, Author, Giving Voice to Values; Formerly Richard M. Waitzer Bicentennial Professor of Ethics, University of Virginia Darden School of Business*

"The authors set out to write this book with the goal of challenging the narrative of successful leadership in the ever-changing context of our times and they have done that in a very compelling way. At its core is an invitation – that there is a need to both 'deconstruct' the past while one finds a way and to 'construct' one's personal agency – the need to be proactive, to create that forward momentum; and yet take people with you while you're on that journey. Anchoring the proposition in the three practices of honest engagement, addressing reality, and adaptive impact makes it a very compelling playbook indeed, inspiring for those who are waiting to author their story while it unfolds around them. Thank you, Jonathan, Frank, and Sudhanshu for leading us into this very important conversation."
— **Adi Sengupta** – *Group Chief Executive, Common Purpose Charitable Trust*

"The authors show us how we can find the pivot point that allows each of us to deliver results beyond results. The invitation is to deliver powerful results with the real gift of followership, sustainability, and human creativity in a digital world."
— **Nick Craig** – *President of Core Leadership Institute, Author of Leading from Purpose*

"For those seeking to lead with significance, foster growth, and sustainable impact, this book is a must-read."
— **Tswelo Kodisang** – *Group Chief People Officer, FirstRand*

Guiding the Tide

In a world increasingly driven by artificial intelligence, leadership needs to move beyond the "agile" approach that dominated organizational leadership practices at the end of the 20th century. What is required now for successful leaders is a skillful juxtaposition of proactivity and humility, which we call "guiding the tide."

Successful leaders of today must demonstrate personal agency in order to guide the tide of events around them rather than have the tide of events sweep them along. The "tide," like a river within an ocean akin to a gulf stream, is a unique, ever-changing stream of business systems, technology, consumers, and competitors.

This book uses storytelling, examples, and clear, everyday language to blend leading-edge psychological research and leadership practices with the authors' own work in coaching, assessing, and developing leaders for three decades around the world. The book takes the reader on a journey through three major learnings:

First, the authors describe the nature of the tide and the demands on leaders to move beyond a reactionary, agile approach toward the forward-leaning, active stance of personal agency.

Second, they describe three critical practices to successfully lead with agency and guide the tide:

- Honest Engagement – the practice of dealing with others from a place of openness, honesty, and a willingness to be vulnerable.
- Addressing Reality – the practice of seeing the world as it is rather than as we wish it to be, the ability to separate fact from fiction and data from desire.
- Adaptive Impact – the practice of driving the organization, team, and oneself forward in a way that creates results-beyond-results, that is, delivering goals while building followership, sustainability and "Humanocity" – the integration of human creativity and judgment with the efficiency of digital automation.

Third, they offer leaders a practical path to achieving the personal agency to successfully guide their organization through the tide that shapes their world.

Guiding the Tide
The Call for Agency in 21st Century Business Leaders

Jonathan Donner
Frank Guglielmo
Sudhanshu Palsule

Routledge
Taylor & Francis Group

A PRODUCTIVITY PRESS BOOK

First published 2025
by Routledge
605 Third Avenue, New York, NY 10158

and by Routledge
4 Park Square, Milton Park, Abingdon, Oxon, OX14 4RN

Routledge is an imprint of the Taylor & Francis Group, an informa business

ISBN: 978-1-032-79424-2 (hbk)
ISBN: 978-1-032-79422-8 (pbk)
ISBN: 978-1-003-49188-0 (ebk)

DOI: 10.4324/9781003491880

Typeset in Minion
by SPi Technologies India Pvt Ltd (Straive)

Contents

Introduction

IN THE BEGINNING...

Leadership is a choice you make. It is neither an entitlement nor a reward for your past successes. It is about making the choice to step into the complex tide of intersecting forces that shape the world in which we operate and guiding it rather than be swept along by it. Ultimately leadership is about two things: who you are and how you show up.

We wrote this book with the goal of challenging the narrative of what successful leadership should look like in a rapidly changing context of the 21st century. What we want to address in these pages is relatively simple: nearly four decades of focus on "agility" as *the* critical leadership skill have resulted in leaders who are too often caught on their back foot – ready to react skillfully to the unexpected, but hesitant to demonstrate agency and guide the future. In other words, they are reactive rather than proactive. Our concern is fundamental: we believe this reactive approach renders leaders ultimately unable to respond successfully to the challenges of today's world. A primary focus on flexibility misreads the reality of today's context by confusing the ability to react – even skillfully – with being a leader.

While the sense of humility engendered by agility is, overall, a positive thing, we believe leaders must be balanced on both feet – leaning forward and ready to shape the future while, at the same time, recognizing that they cannot control everything and will need to be agile and adjust as they go. Our goal with this book is to change the leadership narrative and instigate a shift in perspective, calling on leaders to take two seemingly paradoxical actions: being proactive in creating forward momentum and having the humility to recognize that you can't set a fixed point and align people to it. It is our premise that this shift in perspective will facilitate an active, dynamic new stance for leaders, supported by a higher level of uniquely human-centered skills. We believe this approach offers the most promise for achieving results and creating a positive impact in a world of rapidly accelerating change.

We want to provoke a conversation around the idea that leaders can and should see themselves as the authors of the story unfolding around them, rather than characters driven along by the plot. This form of leadership calls for a skillful juxtaposition of two skills: proactively moving forward and doing so with great humility. We call this approach **guiding the tide**. This, in essence, is what this book is all about: developing personal agency through a combination of proactivity and humility, and helping to develop leaders who can guide the tide of events around them rather than be swept away by those same tides.

Throughout the book we will be using a fictional story of an executive named Maria Miller and her journey through leadership. We will punctuate our content with "Maria Moments," all based on real-life examples from real executives with whom we have had the pleasure of working. These Maria Moments serve to generalize these real-life examples, to maintain the anonymity of the executives and organizations involved, and to showcase these illustrations in a dynamic and engaging setting to make them come alive for the reader.

Why Maria? Maria is an archetype for all of us – well-meaning, sincere, driven, purposeful, and largely successful. We hope you see yourself in Maria and are able to empathize with her. It's likely that you have had experiences that parallel the ones we describe and that you recognize the challenges Maria is confronting. There is one more interesting thing you need to know about Maria. She thinks things through by having imaginary conversations with Frida Kahlo. In the classic epic poem *Paradise Lost*, Dante picked Virgil as his guide to help the reader "hear" his inner thoughts and because Virgil was a vibrant name at the time, someone one could imagine having a vital conversation with. We have positioned Frida Kahlo as Maria's Virgil in this book.

We wish to be clear that we do not see the ideas presented here as lessons drawn directly from Kahlo. Rather, we are using Kahlo as a literary device in order get a glimpse into Maria's thinking. For us, Frida serves the same purpose as Virgil did for Dante, the way Tom Hanks' character spoke to Wilson the Volleyball in the film *Castaway*. Why Frida Kahlo and not an inanimate object? Well, Frida is more interesting, livelier, and certainly lived with more agency than poor Wilson.

THE PLAN OF THE BOOK

We have attempted to write this book in the form of a leadership journey, very much as we see leadership development as a journey. We will follow Maria Miller as she finds her way to guiding the tide and we will join her as she goes through experiences that help define how she comes to practice *Honest Engagement, Addressing Reality,* and *Adaptive Impact.* In Chapter 1, we discuss how the world has changed – not evolved but become completely disrupted – and therefore how we are all called to examine what we think we know about leadership. In Chapter 2, we discuss the tide itself and how leaders can step forward with agency to guide it. In Chapters 3, 4, and 5, we look in depth at the three practices of leading with agency. At each point, we will describe how you can best use these practices.

We will also describe the warning signs and consequences of leading unproductively. We will consolidate these learnings in Chapter 6 where we discuss managing your own journey to developing leadership agency. We will look at one of the most important paradoxes of leaders – the idea that becoming a successful leader can lead you back to the trap of inertia unless you are willing to continually step back from your success, let go of your place of comfort, and step forward into new challenges. In Chapter 7, we will examine the "how" of learning from experience and we will introduce an approach you can adopt throughout your career. We conclude with the Epilogue, reviewing the main points we have made and looking toward the future.

We are three colleagues who have walked divergent but intersecting paths, leading leadership and talent-development functions in major businesses and NGOs, including within the United Nations. We have coached executives across the globe and taught in universities on three continents. Together, we have a combined a century-plus of service helping leaders become leaders. The pandemic, and the world that is emerging from it, led us to a conversation about the future direction of leadership. That conversation led to the book you hold in your hand. Please, join us in the conversation.

Acknowledgments

The ideas that we share here are the culmination of many conversations and interactions with brilliant colleagues and leaders across varied industries around the world. We could never thank them all individually, but collectively they have shaped our thoughts, our experiences, and our approach to leadership.

The execution of this book involved many hands beyond our own. We would like to thank Kristen Weber for her insightful editing, limitless patience, and her uncanny ability to turn our three-part harmony into a single voice. We also would like to thank Jenni Miehle for her creativity in turning our concepts into clear crisp visuals.

Within a few pages, the reader will see that we have chosen a female executive as the protagonist and hero across the stories we use to bring life to our ideas. This is not an accident, as we three men are fortunate to be surrounded by wonderful wives and strong daughters – great role models all. And so, we would like to thank Louise, Claudia, Saumya, Becky, Samantha, Jodi, Sanna Linnea and Sarica Robyn for being our exemplars. No less would we also like to thank our sons, James and Steven, who have found their own ways to step forward into this new century with a sense of personal agency.

Finally, we would like to thank and acknowledge Mary Miller. Mary is an executive of our acquaintance who has led a strong, purposeful, and impactful career. When we set out to write this book, we always tried to keep our audience in mind. Mary was that audience and eventually became the inspiration for our character, Maria Miller, whom you will meet shortly.

About the Authors

Jonathan Donner An internationally recognized expert in senior leadership development, Jonathan Donner has led leadership development efforts at some of the world's most successful global enterprises including Amazon, the UN World Food Programme, Unilever, Altria, and Marks & Spencer.

Frank Guglielmo An executive coach and consultant, Frank Guglielmo has created and led executive development programs, coaching executives across the globe in a wide range of industries. Prior to establishing his own practice, Frank was the head of leadership development at Interpublic Group, Inc. and held senior leadership development roles at several other Fortune 500 companies.

Sudhanshu Palsule An award-winning educator, CEO advisor, and leadership coach, Sudhanshu Palsule is regarded as one of the leading thinkers in the field of transformative leadership. He teaches at Duke Corporate Education and is a Fellow at Cambridge University. His clients include several Fortune 100 companies, governments, and the UN.

1

The Imperatives of 21st-Century Leadership

There are crucial periods in human history when change takes the form not of the usual generational transition, but rather a radical dismantling of the past. We are currently in the grip of such a dismantling. As the world shifts into an unfamiliar reality emerging as the result of the confluence of three gigantic forces: massive digitalization; environmental overshoot; and a deeply polarized world of represented reality,[1] we are witness to unprecedented change. This dismantling is creating its own version of anxiety, with questions around identity, relationships, work, success, happiness, leadership, and purpose. Moreover, this is occurring during a time of growing economic uncertainty, deeply polarized societies, and a world that is being reshaped by generative artificial intelligence (AI). The problems with which we are being routinely challenged are infinitely more complex than those we've faced before.

Most of you (the leaders for whom we wrote this book) were trained by those who came of age in the 20th century with the certainty that came with a relatively stable, post-industrial age. Your expertise and experience came from honing your cognitive and behavioral skills in the solving of complicated problems. Upon these foundations you (and all of us) built stepped, progressively hierarchical careers. The world was perceived as linear, not complex. Your path forward was clear.

Enter Maria Miller...

DOI: 10.4324/9781003491880-1

1

WHERE WE LEARN ABOUT MARIA

Maria Miller is a senior executive at Percipience Ltd., where she holds dual roles. She heads both the new business development group which seeks out new partners, investments, and opportunities, and the customer experience department, housing a global team of 75 responsible for working with existing customers to maximize their use of Percipience Ltd. The company itself provides a range of data services including data mining, analytics, and platform management software.

After graduating from the University of Maryland, Maria joined the sales department of an established cloud computing company. A few years later, she left to get her master's degree at the London School of Economics. This led to a series of roles across companies in the EU and the United States, and eventually Maria became the head of Customer Experience in the EU region for Percipience Ltd. Two years later, she rose to the head of Customer Experience globally, and, last year, New Business Development was added to her portfolio. Most people, including Maria, saw this as a test to determine if she was ready to take on a role in the C-Suite.

Maria is a digital native; someone who has worked in a world in which Internet capabilities, big data, and simple mass communication have always existed. Still, Maria has seen her share of disruptions – the advent of social media, the financial crisis of 2008 (which cost her a promising promotion), Brexit and the kick-off to a new wave of nationalism that dramatically complicated the work of global companies like Percipience Ltd., the Coronavirus pandemic of 2020, and the global upheaval it wrought, all followed by the rapid rise of generative AI.

While working for a multimedia publishing company in London, Maria met and married her husband; a few years later, they had a child. When she was pregnant with her now seven-year-old son, Maria became interested in her heritage and took a home-DNA ancestry test. The results arrived the morning she was hustling off to Paris for a Friday meeting with a plan to spend the weekend. Settling into her seat on the train, she opened the package and was surprised to learn that, among other things, she was 8% Mexican. That weekend, while visiting the Musée National d'Art Moderne, she came across the famous painting·The Frame by the 1930s Mexican surrealist artist Frida Kahlo.

Maria was struck by the painting; it drew her in, and she found herself unable to look away. Having just learned about her own Mexican heritage, Maria began reading up on Kahlo's life and work. She found the artist's life story – like her painting – inspiring and fascinating.

Soon, Maria began to imagine conversations with Frida, especially when working through difficult issues. In a way, Kahlo became Maria's personal muse: a sounding board and a friend. In her quiet moments, Maria would find herself engaged in a lively, imaginary give-and-take with the forceful Kahlo.

Late one evening, Maria Miller sat in her office, thinking about her team's most recent success – they had managed to secure a key sponsorship position for the upcoming Olympics. What a decade this was turning out to be, thought Maria to herself. *The COVID-19 pandemic starting in 2020, the economic turbulence that followed in its wake, the challenge of dealing with new environmental regulations, and, of course, the many struggles to create a more equitable and just world for everybody.*

Out of nowhere, the words, "everybody is reduced to the anxious status of a shady character or a displaced person" *began rattling around in Maria's head. They were from a 1947 poem by W.H. Auden titled "The Age of Anxiety" that had appeared in her social media feed the previous evening. As Maria began to nod off, she heard her office door click open. She looked up and saw Frida Kahlo enter. The artist dropped heavily into a chair.* The "age of anxiety" is a perfect name for the times we are in, *thought Maria.* "Wouldn't you say so, Frida?" she asked.

Frida smiled and nodded. "I can see why you see the similarity." After two world wars, *The Age of Anxiety* became an eponymous description of displacement and the anxiety it brings with it, and the human search for identity in a changing world, *Maria thought grimly.* "The world has been going through a very long and dark tunnel, one several years in the making. It shouldn't have been a surprise that the period of emerging into the sunlight was not going to be easy" *Frida said before adding more lightly,* "But here we are now, and there are things to do."

"Yes," Maria said, smiling. "I miss the time when dealing with what we used to call a VUCA world was all a leader needed to worry about. But it's a new world, time to get to work."

There is no doubt that the world has become significantly more complex, as well as ambiguous, uncertain, and volatile. Digital technology is taking apart the world as we knew it; this is just the beginning of a long phase of continuous disruption. A new reality of a hyper-transparent, globally networked world is upon us. In the next handful of years, we are likely to see more changes brought about by digitalization than we have experienced over the past century. After all, we are just scratching the surface of AI.

We believe that to lead successfully in this new complex world, leaders need to have a sense of personal **agency**. Leaders must see themselves as the authors of the story unfolding around them – however complex and different it may be – rather than characters driven along by the plot. It is for this reason that we are introducing the term, "Guiding the Tide." Think of "the tide" like a river within an ocean, akin to the Gulf Stream in the Atlantic. The tide is the unique but ever-changing stream of systems, technology, society, consumers, and competitors, powered by human energy. It is always found within the larger ocean of economic, social, political, physical, and environmental forces (Figure 1.1).

Guiding the tide is how you can exercise agency in a complex, uncertain, 21st-century context. Leading with agency to guide the tide requires combining proactive steps forward with great humility. As we will elaborate

FIGURE 1.1
Guiding the Tide

later, guiding the tide requires leaders to build capabilities in three "practices":

1. Honest Engagement
2. Addressing Reality
3. Adaptive Impact

Failing to do so can result in a leader falling into three corresponding leadership traps:

1. Transactional façade
2. Deluded certitude
3. Stuck in neutral

This book is about developing these three practices and avoiding the corresponding traps. As you read through the remaining chapters in this book, you will follow Maria Miller's journey as she comes to terms with the demands of leadership in a 21st-century context. With Frida by her side, she examines her choices, learns from her mistakes, and seeks to guide the tide in this brave, new world of leadership.

WHERE DID THE 20TH CENTURY GO? I SWEAR IT WAS HERE A MINUTE AGO...[2]

But before we begin, we must take a couple of steps back. When Maria wondered if the title of Auden's poem "The Age of Anxiety" would be an apt description for today, she wasn't far from the mark even if the sense of displacement and the sources of anxiety are considerably different than when Auden was writing.

Certainty, control, and predictability were terms that signified an age in which linear was the ideal. Given a set of coordinates, you could, with reasonable confidence, plot your five-year plan along that line. Knowing what to do when faced with a challenge was easy if you had the requisite "competencies" and the experience demanded by the job. So, strategy was king in the kingdom of certainty, and the S-curve the holy grail. For those of you who went to a business school in the 1990s, it was more than likely you had a strategy professor waxing eloquent about the S-curve, especially the top of the curve when the flat line meant stability. Our love affair with a linear world continued well into the later years of the 20th century.

As long as the world stayed relatively stable, our assumption of linearity appeared more than justified.

However, the storm was already brewing, and it was only a matter of time before it would land on the shores of the 21st century. Join us on a whistle-stop tour through six key factors that went into the making of the storm.

Greed Disguised as Market Economics

The business world reeled from the collapse of Enron in 2001 as well as from the web of deceit and lies surrounding it. The years between 2001 and 2007 saw two developments with far-reaching consequences on the world. The first was the most severe worldwide economic crisis since the Great Depression of the 1930s. What began in the United States with the subprime mortgage crisis and the continuous build-up of toxic assets in banks spread quickly to Europe and eventually led to the collapse of the Greek and Icelandic economies. According to the International Monetary Fund, large U.S. and European banks lost more than $1 trillion in suddenly worthless assets between 2007 and 2009 as markets collapsed. Greed – it became clear – had become the new byword in the financial industry, and living life beyond one's means was the easy mantra. Unbridled market economics had assumed a life of its own, unmoored from most humanistic considerations. The societal wealth gap continued to grow, with the tax on wealth contributing a mere four cents on the dollar while, according to Oxfam, half the world continued to subsist on less than $5.50 per day.[3]

Massive Digitalization

The second big development was the coming of the age of digitalization, which reached a critical turning point around 2004 with computing speeds and storage capacities reaching an inflection point, generating the beginning of the Internet of Things. From Facebook to LinkedIn, most social media platforms began in some stage around this time. As we completed the writing of this book, generative AI is beginning to sweep the globe. Universities are rushing to set up new rules, businesses are trying to figure out the opportunities and the risks, and governments are scrambling to establish new regulations. However, this is still just version 2.0. After two more iterations, we are likely to see the full muscle power of a multi-modal AI that can work with a trillion parameters and interact with human beings through speech and perform tasks on command. Yuval Harari, writing in

The Guardian (24 May 2017), alerted the world to the rise of the "useless class," created by computers that outperform humans. Organizations and employees are both excited and intimidated by what lies ahead.

Dehumanized Work

Generative AI notwithstanding, the fact is that the lack of meaningful work continues to be a source of dehumanization in countless workplaces globally. Anthropologist David Graeber wrote in his 2018 book, *Bullshit Jobs* (Allen Lane), that half of the work done in the world is pointless and psychologically destructive in a context where work is associated with self-worth. The New Economics Foundation published research by Eilis Lawlor, Helen Kersley, and Susan Reed that compared the salaries of professions at the top and bottom of the pay scale with the social value of these jobs, taking into account their impact on communities and the environment. They found that city bankers, while earning salaries between $750,000 and $15m, destroy $15 of social value for every dollar in value they generate. A well-paid advertising executive destroys $20 of value for each dollar they get paid, while a hospital cleaner creates over $7 in social value. Clearly, this is an unsustainable strategy for the business world to continue following.

Environmental Overshoot

Around the same time, global warming reached approximately 1°C above pre-industrial levels in 2017.[4] In just six years, that has climbed to 1.45 degrees C, according to the World Meteorological Report of 2023, record high ocean temperatures made the news in 2023 signaling that the capacity of the oceans to absorb heat is under severe strain. Climate change with its many ramifications has severe debilitating effects on the business world. According to the CDP Global Supply Chain report, climate change alone accounts for 93% of the total environmental costs for business.[5]

A World Fragmented and Polarized

Alongside all these developments, the global social landscape was becoming increasingly polarized, with social media adding a brand-new dimension to hyper-partisan behavior. Does social media push people apart? "Yes," says Chris Bail from Duke University in his 2021 book, *Breaking the Social Media Prism: How to Make Our Platforms Less Polarizing* (Princeton).

Where once it was thought that social media would connect the world and democratize our voices, we've learned that it is, in fact, much more complicated. "Post-truth" became a legitimate term and a new reality of divisiveness and intolerance began sweeping across the globe. New social clusters began to form with unlikely bedfellows like climate change deniers and the socio-economically disenfranchised; and politics became increasingly more manipulative and fragmented. Social media has played a key role in manipulating elections, fostering a new muscular form of nationalism through a breed of plutocratic leaders, slowly but surely altering the world at the level of geo-politics and societies.

And Then the Pandemic

As we mentioned in the Introduction, we wrote this book against the backdrop of the pandemic, which became the spark that ignited many of these forces and pushed us into a dark tunnel, dismantling our lives and work. Terms like "reset" and "the new normal" became clumsy clichés that attempted to make sense of a new reality. Deserted city streets, empty office towers, and shuttered businesses across the globe cast a ghostly, dystopian shadow over a human species whose fragility had been suddenly exposed. C-Suite teams scrambled to reset their course over video calls that ran late into the night, economists rushed to offer their prognoses on the coming boom or recession, and politicians continued to posture in mock confidence, blaming everyone but themselves.

The pandemic was simply the last component in the perfect storm, the culmination of many factors that had been quietly gathering momentum until they reached a head. A 2020 *New York Times* article by Thomas Friedman captured it aptly with the headline, *"How we broke the world."* Overshooting the sustainable limits of the planet's life-support systems; living far beyond our means by borrowing more than we can ever pay back; disregarding the societal wealth gap and the consequent dehumanization of millions; a world so polarized and driven by a growing discourse of intolerance and hatred; and an utter disregard for what makes us human: these are but a few of the items on a much longer list of what broke the world.

Comfortably Numb

But this book is not intended to be about the making of the perfect storm, and neither are we qualified to write about issues concerning technology or geo-politics. The impulse for this book began as a conversation between the three of us in early 2020 over a few Espresso Martinis in a Cambridge, MA, bar just before the pandemic lockdowns. We spoke about the compassion we felt for the leaders that we knew and admired who were clearly struggling. We came to the epiphany that, as leaders, *"we've just got too comfortably numb."*

Nothing illustrates the "comfortably numb" condition better than the appropriation of the acronym VUCA. To leaders and leadership development geeks, the origin story of the well-known concept of VUCA or *Volatile, Uncertain, Complex*, and *Ambiguous* is the stuff of lore. In 1987, as the implications for military leadership at the end of the Cold War became increasingly apparent, a crack group of military scholars was assembled to craft a new leadership view. This elite task force characterized the emerging context for leadership as volatile, uncertain, complex, and ambiguous.

Since then, VUCA made its way into the world of business, and it soon became customary to use the term every time a non-linear situation with multiple variables arose. It became so ubiquitous that VUCA has gone on to find a prominent place in contemporary leadership discourse. There is no doubt that VUCA has prompted several important and constructive developments in leadership theory including the recognition of humility as an important mindset, the limitations of top-down leadership, the importance of intelligent risk taking, the dangers of arrogant certainty, and the concept of agility, to name but a few. It has, among other things, challenged traditional approaches to planning and helped to evolve new approaches and models of non-hierarchical leadership.

However – and this is our big sticking point – while VUCA has shaped the leadership narrative in many positive ways, it has also effectively stunted its evolution. In our observation, as leaders began to embrace the unpredictable leadership context of a VUCA world, the term also inadvertently became a proxy for a somewhat fatalistic approach to the new complex reality. Labeling a complex situation as VUCA made it easy to simply accept the situation as such, and consequently, it diminished the imperative to act! This is not a productive strategy; rather, it is a retreat from the imperatives of true leadership, which are centered around Agency!

Becoming Irrelevant

The seeming lack of *agency* in leadership is something we have been noticing for a while now. Leadership has a long history punctuated and prompted by individuals and groups who have stepped forward decisively into their reality with a deep and personal conviction that they can and must effect the change they seek to bring about. These leaders have demonstrated the type of leadership that embraces reality, with a sense of vision and clarity that cuts through the apathy and inertia of their organizational, political, and economic contexts. Then why do we see such a lack of Agency? What is it about the 21st century and its complex set of problems that has numbed our leadership?

The philosopher Jean Huston spoke of the problem of leadership as being "ill prepared to deal with the chaos and complexity of today's world where too much is happening too quickly."[6] Yes, the problems that abound daily are far more complex than ever before. Yes, they are also appearing more rapidly and at a scale that we have not seen before. Unpredictable geo-political issues and conflicts, currency fluctuations, and wildly erratic commodity prices are just a few of the multiple unknowns that go into making the many complex systems we must deal with. During the time we spent writing this book, the world has seen the onset of two ongoing wars, floods, earthquakes, political changes, and social unrest! This is just the world outside; the context in which we operate.

On top of all this, there is a myriad of uncertainties much closer to home beginning with all the internal tangles inside your organization that get in the way of quick decision-making, responding in a timely nature to external changes, and motivating your own people. Customers have more choices than ever before and easy access to information – no longer a source of competitive advantage for you. Technology has created a level playing field whether you are a hundred-year-old company or a start-up. Your own list of challenges may be even more varied.

Where Do We Go from Here?

Unfortunately, there is no magic bullet to leading with Agency in a complex 21st century. However hard and complex it gets, leaders must step forward into their environment and guide the tide of life events. In fact, it is when we are truly being tested, when either our assumptions about the world are challenged by a new reality or the methods we have learned to use are no longer working, that we experience maximum potential for growth.

We are collectively experiencing a time in which our Industrial Age principles and ways of working are being dismantled by a new 21st-century reality. In particular, so many of our assumptions about leadership, especially about hierarchies, structure, status, power, and roles are being challenged by a new reality that does not adhere to Industrial Age principles. Just calling it VUCA and numbing our leadership is not the answer. What a perfect time for change! If we can learn to build new narratives for ourselves – narratives that allow us to guide the tide of life events – we can successfully execute our efforts to navigate in this new reality.

IT'S ABOUT: GUIDING THE TIDE

Guiding the tide is a leader's capacity to engage with their environment realistically and productively. Three practices lie at the heart of a leader's ability to guide the tide (Figure 1.2).

Honest Engagement calls for dealing with others from a place of openness, honesty, and a willingness to be vulnerable. This is foundational to building productive followership. A failure to practice Honest Engagement results in what we call *Transactional Façade*, the inclination to mold one's purpose, values, and mental framework to meet the anticipated desires of others, or of the situation one finds oneself in. Transactional façade involves constantly shifting one's core beliefs and values to the demands of the moment.

Addressing Reality requires leaders to see the world as it is rather than as they wish it to be; the ability to separate fact from fiction and data from desire. This allows for a recognition of what outcomes are truly

| HONEST ENGAGEMENT | ADDRESSING REALITY | ADAPTIVE IMPACT |

FIGURE 1.2
Guiding the Tide Practices

of value to an organization. A failure to Address Reality results in what we call *Deluded Certitude* – substituting one's desired state for reality, seeing the world through the lens of what one wants to be true, rather than following the evidence and information.

Adaptive Impact is the practice of stepping into the tide in order to successfully lead the organization, team, and yourself forward in a way that creates sustainable success and ongoing relevance. A failure to practice Adaptive Impact results in what we call *Stuck in Neutral* – clinging to the status quo and formerly successful approaches to avoid or delay moving into a new, uncertain world.

These three practices – Honest Engagement, Addressing Reality, and Adaptive Impact – support the ability to look beyond immediate targets and goals. They allow a leader to step forward toward long-term viability and accountability to a larger set of constituents in their ecosystems. Leaders who can "guide the tide" create the capacity to carry their organization forward in the face of continual disruption, unrelating complexity, and the fog of ambiguity.

- *Honest Engagement* provides you with an anchor, so that you are not swept away by the tide and phenomena outside your control.
- *Addressing Reality* allows you to see the shape and direction of the tide, thereby guiding your actions.
- *Adaptive Impact* gives you the tools to guide the direction of the tide toward your intent.

Guiding the tide successfully provides leaders with the opportunity to achieve results-beyond-results, the realization of a level of leadership impact that is not only recognized and respected, but importantly, that addresses what is required for leading in the 21st century. Specifically, results-beyond-results refers to delivering critical outcomes beyond the achievement of specific business targets such as:

- *Followership: Coalescing human energy*
  Building a direction and a momentum that others seek to follow, goals that others wish to adopt, and a vision that others want to share.

- *Sustainability: Driving renewable value*
  Delivering value in a way that outpaces the resources consumed and continually exploring innovative ways of crafting the future.
- *Humanocity: Creating meaning for individuals and the ecosystem*
  Finding ways to integrate human creativity with technological efficiency to create meaning in a world increasingly dominated by digital technology.

The 21st century in all its emergence and unfolding presents us with a powerful call to action to rethink and reimagine the approaches we take to leadership. The time is now. It is clear that we cannot continue leading from the reactive leadership approach that predominated at the dawn of the digital age. The writing appeared on the wall a while ago, but the heady momentum of the past continued well beyond its usefulness. The signals from the future are already here and they are imploring us to act decisively. We believe leaders can make the choice to step into the swirling tide and show up with the agency that guides the future in a positive, productive direction. We are optimistic that we are about to take an important step in the evolution of leadership. In the next chapter, we begin this journey.

NOTES

1 We are using the term "represented reality" to describe an extended post-truth world characterized by social noise, diminishing attention, and fragmentation.
2 Songwriters: John E Prine/Steve Goodman. The Twentieth Century Is Almost Over lyrics © BMG Rights Management, Downtown Music Publishing, Sony/ATV Music Publishing LLC.
3 C. Coffey, "Time to Care: Unpaid and Underpaid Care Work and the Global Inequality Crisis" (Oxford: Oxfam International, 2020).
4 IPCC, *Global Warming of 1.5°C: IPCC Special Report on Impacts of Global Warming of 1.5°C above Pre-Industrial Levels in Context of Strengthening Response to Climate Change, Sustainable Development, and Efforts to Eradicate Poverty*, 1st ed. (Cambridge University Press, 2022), https://doi.org/10.1017/9781009157940.
5 "Transparency to Transformation: A Chain Reaction," Company Report, CDP Global Supply Chain Report 2020 (CDP Global Supply Chain Program, February 2021), https://cdn.cdp.net/cdp-production/cms/reports/documents/000/005/554/original/CDP_SC_Report_2020.pdf?1614160765.
6 Jean Houston, *Being a Social Artist*, Audio Recording, n.d., https://www.awakin.org/v2/read/view.php?op=audio&tid=424.

2

Learning to Guide the Tide

WHERE MARIA LEARNS THAT SHE HAS GROWN

Maria Miller pulled into the car park at her office building. Normally, it was a treat for her to be coming into the office – something she did only four or five times a month – today, however was different. She had a difficult conversation ahead of her.

Twenty minutes later, Maria settled into the office she would be using for the day. She was sipping her second coffee when Jason stuck his head in. "Are we ready to meet?" he asked.

"Yes, Jason, come on in and close the door," Maria said with a tight smile.

Jason walked in. He was 36 years old, wearing horn-rimmed glasses and, for once, a shirt with a collar rather than one of the retro tee shirts he favored.

Jason sat down. "I'm confused, and I must say, a bit upset," he said quietly. "Frankly, I was stunned yesterday when Michelle told me my job is ending and I'll be leaving the company in two weeks. I wanted to meet with you to see if there were any options to find a different role for me. I enjoy it here and have always been told I'm a valued member of the team."

Maria took a deep breath. Jason is – or was – a team leader in the customer experience organization heading a group that focused on helping customers with Percipience Ltd.'s oldest product: a data analytics tool that produces consumer metrics dashboards. Two years ago, at Maria's recommendation, the company announced it would stop investing in the product and, six months ago, customers and staff were informed that support would

DOI: 10.4324/9781003491880-2

be outsourced from Percipience Ltd. All of the developers and most of the customer experience staff had moved on to other roles. A few were let go. Initially, Jason had received offers from several other product groups, but he had not been interested. He'd told his manager Michelle that he wanted to continue to work with his customer, Persuasion Marketing, a major client and one of the largest customers still using the product.

"Jason," Maria said, "we have been clear all along that we are moving away from Dashboard Dynamics. Everyone else has moved to new roles. I know you love the team at Persuasion, but we see that product as obsolete and are moving strongly into our new AI-driven dashboards. Haven't you been listening to our internal podcasts?" she asked sympathetically.

"Of course," said Jason, "but I talk to my customers all the time and they're committed to this product. It's part of their infrastructure and they're sticking with it. They were always big business for us, so I wanted to continue to help them."

"The writing has been on the wall," Maria said. "How could you miss it? We bought an AI company two years ago and our engineers have been rebuilding our analytics capability based on that acquisition. We made a major product announcement and have been offering everyone working on the legacy product the chance to interview in other groups. Two months ago, we signed an outsourcing support deal to maintain the product for the few clients who didn't want to transition, including Persuasion. Didn't you know all of this?" Maria was a bit exasperated.

"I spoke with the team at Persuasion who I've been working with for years," Jason said. "They assured me they have no plans to replace the dashboards they have. I reviewed the backlog of work we have with them and there's enough work for at least another year. I don't understand why I can't just keep delivering. We bill them for my work, we make money. I don't get it." Jason was clearly mystified.

"Jason, you are a talented guy, but this is over," Maria said clearly. "You've had six months to find a new role and you chose not to do so. I know this will be hard to hear right now but let me give you some advice. As you move through your career, it is important that you address reality and see things the way they are – not how you wish them to be. You need to be thoughtful about where you get information and who you listen to. Take it from me, you need to seek information from multiple sources and not rely on one voice." Maria rose from her chair and extended her hand. "Best of luck to you. Please stay in touch." Jason left unhappily.

As the door closed behind him, Maria thought grumpily, Well, that went well. Oh, Frida, why is it that some people can be so blind? *As usual, Maria was conjuring Frida Kahlo.*

With a twinkle in her eye, Frida said, "Take it from an artist, perceiving the world is not always the easiest thing. I can remember at least one up-and-coming young executive who let her own certitude blind her to reality."

Frida took Maria back to 2008, a year after she'd graduated from college and was working hard at her first job at a cloud computing company. "Maria, think back," Frida said. "You were selling cloud computing services and focusing on several mid- and large-sized banks as clients. The news was filled with stories of a financial crisis, the U.S. government was looking for ways to avoid a depression, and all of your sales prospects were making statements intended to assure customers that they were going to take steps to remain solvent. Your boss was telling you to develop leads in other sectors. But no. You were so certain that you knew what you were doing. The circle of people you listened to started to shrink until you were mostly just talking to the IT people running the RFPs, the same people deeply invested in keeping the potential projects going. When all of their companies pulled the plug on the cloud service transitions to save cash, you were totally blindsided. You missed all of your sales targets and lost the promotion you were chasing. I seem to recall you quit immediately after that."

True, *thought Maria.* But at least it got me to London and life worked out. And I learned to see things as they are rather than be blinded by my belief that I was right.

"Yes. A good lesson but a hard way to learn it. Let's hope Jason figures it out," said Frida as she faded from Maria's thoughts.

And So

As we saw with Jason, the company's decision to end the product line that had made him successful in the past was a critical experience. As Maria explained, reality had sent Jason many signals, but rather than engage with those signals, he had chosen to settle into the comfort of his belief that his past success would insulate him. At the same time, we saw that Maria was willing to lead the company away from a successful, but outdated product and toward a new product offering – despite the reticence of some customers. Maria was guiding the tide on which her company was competing, shaping the people, processes, and purpose to make them successful. She refused to be stuck in neutral (trying to drive a familiar strategy) and demonstrated her willingness to drive the execution of a new product. Finally, we watched Jason trying to adopt the façade that he believed the company wanted – a loyal soldier, while Maria approached him with honesty about her values as well as those of the company.

This chapter will deliver our blueprint of the what, how, and why for leaders to step into the tide with agency to deliver results-beyond-results. First, we introduce the concept of the tide and point out the obvious – that today leaders live in, deal with, and lead through complexity. We then introduce what we see as the critical "practices" for stepping into the tide with a sense of agency – a belief that you can shape the flow of events rather than be driven by them. We will take a moment to explain each of these three practices and how to make them part of your leadership approach. We conclude the chapter with a discussion of how you can develop these practices.

LEADERSHIP AND THE TIDE

The challenges facing leaders today are profoundly different than those faced by past generations. The volume, pace, scale, and interconnectivity of forces around us are no longer simply factors to address, but the context within which we lead. They are a tide that we swim within. By "the Tide" we are referring to the unique but ever-changing stream of systems, technology, society, consumers, and competitors, powered by human energy, within the larger ocean of economic, social, political, physical, and environmental forces. Leading within the tide removes the luxury of having a playbook, or of sitting back and reacting. Leaders can shape, or guide the tide but cannot control it. Think about the agency of the single protester in Tiananmen Square – how that powerful image changed the direction of civil protest in Asia. Living and leading within complexity – rather than *responding* to complexity – requires a sense of agency, which is essential to guiding the tide. Let's begin by looking into the nature of complexity in the 21st century.

The Nature of 21st-Century Complexity

"The future will reward clarity but punish certitude."[1] Bob Johansen's telling quote is a stark reminder of what works and what doesn't in complex

circumstances. Certitude is a great place to be in; it is the comfort zone. There, we feel competent, just as Jason did, and we know for sure that we have the expertise and experience to solve whatever problems come our way. Yes, as long as the problems that come our way are the kind we've solved before. Certitude can be an effective state of mind for dealing with complicated problems. The thing about complicated problems is that once we know the solution, we get better at it through repeated practice. This is true if the problem itself does not change much. That is what makes expertise and experience such great allies!

However, when we are dealing with complex problems that are not amenable to what we know, certitude becomes a problem. Now we must learn, which sounds easier than it is, because learning means challenging our established ways of thinking that have been successful up to this point, as well as our beliefs that have led us this far. Novelty requires an entirely different approach beginning with the profound acceptance that, "*I may not know the answer at all.*" It becomes increasingly difficult to adopt this state of mind with success and authority!

But what exactly is complexity? The short answer is this: a complex system is (1) **self-organizing** in that it consists of multiple variables and agents, and each of those take decisions that you cannot control; (2) the system is **adaptive** as the multiple variables and agents keep interacting with each other; you are not in charge of these interactions; and (3) as a result, the system is highly **emergent** and unpredictable. Is the world in which we operate today much more complex than it was before? Yes. The very nature of an interconnected and interdependent world on a global scale made possible by digital technology is far more complex than anything we have known before. As we said in the previous chapter, the complex systems we face on a routine basis are what we call the tide: the unique but ever-changing stream of systems, technology, society, consumers, and competitors.

The problem – as we know only too well – is the way we approach complexity. Nature in her infinite wisdom ensured that the human brain has a built-in energy conservation system – habits and default patterns that keep us anchored to what we know best. Building habits that help us stick to a winning strategy was a great survival tool in a time when the dangers were obvious. Less so in a digital and entangled environment. On top of that, our entire 20th-century orientation – both in education and in management – has favored what Heifetz, Linsky, and Grashow refer to as solving "*technical problems*" rather than responding to "*adaptive challenges.*"[2]

According to Heifetz and his colleagues, solving technical problems means focusing on resolving the immediate challenge, while adaptive problem-solving involves creating systemic change by addressing the underlying context that created the problem in the first place. All in all, we aren't well-positioned to deal with complexity as we think we are.

Now, Jason's error was in not picking up the signals that were coming at him because he was so comfortably ensconced in his world of expertise and experience. Hopefully, this situation will serve as an important watershed moment for his development. The real challenge for you, however, is what happens when you are in a position of leadership and you must lead your team and organization by guiding the tide that is ebbing and flowing in unpredictable ways.

GUIDING THE TIDE PRACTICES

This is where the practices that support a leaders' ability to guide the tide become relevant. The model below outlines the backbone of the approach we are proposing for 21st-century leaders (Figure 2.1).

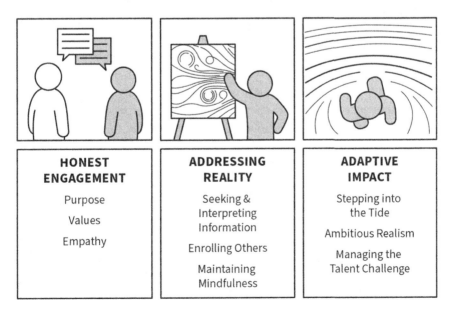

HONEST ENGAGEMENT	ADDRESSING REALITY	ADAPTIVE IMPACT
Purpose Values Empathy	Seeking & Interpreting Information Enrolling Others Maintaining Mindfulness	Stepping into the Tide Ambitious Realism Managing the Talent Challenge

FIGURE 2.1
Guiding the Tide Practices

1. **Honest Engagement**:

   Honest Engagement is the bedrock of the leadership approach we are discussing. It is what successful leaders use to ground themselves amidst the constant motion of the driving tide. It begins with a deep understanding of who you are and how you relate to the world. You can build this understanding with an exploration of the three foundations of your identity: your purpose, your core values, and your ability to relate to the world through a function called empathy.

   - **Purpose** – Clarifying what you are trying to achieve in your role and with your life.
   - **Values** – Establishing how you will judge the appropriateness of your ends and means.
   - **Empathy** – Understanding what a situation or person calls upon you to do.

     Drawing productive lessons from experiences that allow you to understand your purpose and your values, and explore how you relate to the world helps develop the capacity for *Honest Engagement*. As you can imagine, this is a lifelong learning experience!

2. **Addressing Reality**:

   Addressing Reality is about the choices you must make about how you interact with that world. Ultimately, it requires the ability to see the world as it is, rather than how you wish it to be; achieving the ability to separate fact from fiction and data from desire. This, of course, is a major personal developmental leap as well as a challenge. To build this practice, you will have to make the conscious effort to pause and ask questions about the quality of attention that you bring to your interactions with the world. How do you seek and interpret information? How do you enroll others to create a shared understanding of the world and the future? How do you stay mindful about what is important? You can enhance your development of this practice through a focus on:

   - **Seeking and Interpreting Information** – Managing your biases to make sense of information in a fact-based, evidence-driven manner to see what is going on around you.
   - **Enrolling Others** – Involving others actively in creating a joint understanding of the world that guides your action and judgment.
   - **Maintaining Mindfulness** – Remaining focused on what is crucial now while at the same time, keeping your attention on the full

field, seeing over the horizon, and recognizing your own impact on the situation.

3. **Adaptive Impact**:

Adaptive Impact is the practice of stepping into the tide in order to drive the organization, team, and oneself forward in a way that creates sustainable success and ongoing relevance. Leaders build this practice through:

- **Stepping into the Tide** – locating the critical pivot point where the complex components of the tide intersect and creating a meaningful disruption to shape the flow.
- **Embodying Ambitious Realism** – helping others come together to define an ambitious future that is both grounded in reality and worth striving for by everyone the leader leads.
- **Meeting the Talent Challenge** – ensuring that you and those around you remain continually relevant to meet the challenges on the horizon.

This book will provide you with extensive opportunities to understand these concepts more deeply and practically. However, at this point, it may be useful to summarize these concepts in the following manner: Honest Engagement is the personal and grounded stance that we take to the world around us; Addressing Reality is the lens of understanding through which we engage the world; and Adaptive Impact is what we "do" to make a difference for ourselves, others, and the world.

Developing Honest Engagement – The Challenge of Understanding Myself and My Relationship with the World

All leadership development is first and foremost a process of self-discovery. Awareness – if properly directed – shines a light not only on who we are but on who we can become. As Joseph Campbell wrote so evocatively, *"The privilege of a lifetime is to become who you truly are."*[3] The process of self-discovery is more about stripping away what we are not, rather than making additions to what we are. It puts us in the mind of Michelangelo's answer about how he created David, his marble masterpiece that stands tall in the Accademia Gallery in Florence. *"I only took away the parts that were not David,"* he reportedly said about his magnificent creation.

In the act of stripping away, we begin to reveal the three foundational elements of knowing ourselves: *Purpose, Values,* and the supporting role of *Empathy.*

Purpose

Purpose consists of the desires, imagined futures, and hoped-for contributions we believe we can bring into being over the course of our lives. Purpose is your reason for doing what you do; your reason for being. It is a bigger concept than what we typically think of as motivation. Purpose is a targeted, focused question that asks: What is the role of this organization, this department, this group, myself in this place and time? Purpose answers the question: What is the unique contribution I wish to make and what impact do I seek to create to make our world a better place?[4]

Values

Values are judgments that we hold: they can be either about the desirability of an end state (terminal values), or the appropriateness of a way of achieving a goal (values in action).[5] End state or terminal values help us prioritize outcomes. You may value some outcomes more than others because they align with your purpose. *"Values in action"* shape how we approach tasks, conversations, and problems. You may value certain approaches over others because they align with your purpose. Values provide a meaningful context to our behaviors, actions, and conversations.

If purpose and value are the keys to understanding ourselves, then the function that allows us to understand how we relate to the world is empathy.

Empathy

Empathy is having a positive and productive cognitive, emotional, and behavioral response to others. In other words, how do we understand what a situation or person calls upon us to do? Giving a positive cognitive (or rational) response to someone means seeking to know them and taking the time to learn about their goals, agendas, challenges, and capabilities. The emotional component of empathy allows you to be curious about their values and purpose, with openness and without judgment. In other words, to be able to "feel where they are coming from." Caring about someone is the behavioral aspect of empathy. It is a willingness to engage in efforts to help further another person's purpose within the context of their goals, agendas, and constraints. Empathy, of course, is not limited to the reaction you have to another person; it can be applied to other groups or organizations as well.

What Is the Challenge That Must Be Resolved in Understanding Oneself?

Ultimately, to know the world, you must first know yourself. The core challenge you face when confronted with moments of understanding yourself is to resolve these questions of purpose and values in a productive way. This means, understanding who you are for yourself, and not for others. The core challenge that empathy presents is that of shutting off the internal noise in our brains so that we can tune in to listening to the other, be that a person or a situation.

Through the productive resolution of this challenge, you can learn to **engage** with the world **honestly**. Approaching the world *honestly* allows leaders to be themselves – to be vulnerable, open, and to connect in a way that remains consistent across the vagaries of day-to-day obstacles. To *engage* means to close the social distance between yourself and others, to work jointly toward common ends. The capacity for Honest Engagement is the result of resolving the challenge of "Knowing Myself" such that you identify and accept a purpose to life, establish values that align with this purpose, and create an "empathic framework" that allows you to see yourself within a complex system.

The unproductive resolution of the challenge of "understanding myself" is what we call **Transactional Façade**. A Transactional Façade is one in which a leader regularly shifts how they see themselves in order to meet the demands of the moment. It is a way of leading in which a leader tries to match their conversations, actions, and behaviors to a perception of what they think others desire. It requires you to constantly re-invent yourself to match the moment and deal with others on a transactional basis. In other words, trying to be everything for everyone. A second version of the transactional façade is where we cocoon ourselves inside a hardened, narcissistic shell that no one can penetrate, forcing those around us to continuously adapt to us. Such leaders usually leave a trail of disaster.[6]

Moving Forward toward Agency

Engaging honestly with others (what some authors have called "authenticity") has been recognized as an attribute of successful leadership for quite some time. However, authenticity and even purpose can only serve as a foundation; the critical components inherent in impactful leaders are about *action, execution,* and *impact.* With Honest Engagement as a foundation, guiding the tide requires leaders to address reality and continually adjust their approach accordingly for sustained adaptive impact. This is a clear shift away from looking at one's internal self or *insight* – to looking at the world around you, what Herminia Ibarra[7] labels *"outsight."* It is a fundamental and empowering aspect of the evolution toward Leadership Agency.

Addressing Reality – The Challenge of Truly Perceiving the World

Perceiving the world constitutes a pivot away from an internal focus to external orientation. As explained earlier, the challenge is to perceive the world accurately enough to be able to see situations as they really are, rather than how we wish them to be. This involves being sharply aware of the heuristics and belief systems that hijack your perceptual abilities. It also pushes us to avoid interpreting what we perceive through the narrow lenses of bias, culture, and habit. Addressing Reality is an act of choice about three things: how to seek and interpret information, how we enroll others, and how we remain mindful.

Seeking and Interpreting Information

"We don't see things as they are, but as we are," goes an old pronouncement on the fallibility of the human mind, outlining a tendency to project our beliefs and biases rather than see things as they are. Information seeking therefore must involve an active effort directed toward seeking out multiple credible sources rather than passively accepting ideas. It is the difference between seeking out reliable data versus acting on anecdote, or worse, sources on social media! Alfred Korzybski's[8] iconic statement, *"The map is not the territory,"* reveals the limitation of the maps we carry around in our heads. A map works well in a more stable, slower-paced, and linear world, whereas in a complex and changing landscape, maps need to be redrawn time and again. Seeking information then, from a leadership perspective, is about being proactive and fluid in the ways we access information.

Once we perceive information, we quickly interpret it based on our worldview. The challenge of interpretation is that we try and create meaning by fitting what we perceive into a predetermined set of rules, norms, and beliefs we carry with us. Using these pre-set assumptions about how the world works gives us a sense of certitude and control when interpreting new information. However, realistically interpreting information requires that you assess the data you've acquired with judgment grounded in critical reason rather than in emotion or prior beliefs. In other words, you must actively avoid what social scientists call "confirmation bias." This can be especially difficult on self-curated places like social media where we – unwillingly or not – create our own personal echo chambers, reverberating our beliefs back to us. The challenge is to accept ambiguity and relinquish the need for certitude and control. Operating in ambiguity is hard, as it challenges deeply ingrained neural circuits in the human brain that are rewarded for reaching closure.

Enrolling Others in a Common Ambition

Enrolling Others means truly bringing others together in the way they see the world as it is today and the potential they see for how it can be tomorrow. There are three critical activities that you must engage in to successfully enroll others to form a shared perspective of common purpose. First is to accept that the task is to create a joint understanding of the world, rather than bringing others around to your way of understanding. This requires seeing others' views as intrinsically valuable and allowing their perspective to become equal to your own. Second, you must foster the use of this common understanding to guide the actions and judgments of everyone by fully connecting with the needs and motivations of others. Finally, you must make the future present right now, helping others to take action based on a common shared vision of what the future could be.

Remaining Mindful to Be Aware

Mindfulness is about actively choosing to: live in the present, see the whole field, peer over the horizon, and recognize our own impact on the situation – all at once. The role of awareness in the human brain is to allow for clarity without having to commit to certainty. Mindfulness can create pathways for you to remain open to possibilities and make a choice about a decision, rather than be subjected to the brain's need for closure. Remaining mindful is a way of escaping the gravitational pull of automatic mental processes. We've all had the experience of driving down a familiar highway and then "snapping to" and realizing we have no memory of the past 20 minutes.

We were driving on "automatic." Now imagine being in an all-too-familiar meeting – how many of our reactions, questions, and interpretations are "automatic?" The answer depends on our degree of mindfulness.

What Is the Challenge That Must Be Resolved in Addressing Reality?

Experiences that challenge you to "perceive the world" require Addressing Reality by enrolling others to mindfully seek and interpret information in a way that allows us to see the world as it is, not how we wish it to be. This is a deeply humbling experience, one in which you approach the world willfully naïve and ready to adapt, adjust, and change your views based on the truth. It can mean a willingness to admit to blind spots and failure, setting aside ego in pursuit of what is truly valuable and needed by your followers, organization, and, at times, society at large. From a developmental perspective, this also means consciously choosing situations that challenge us, spending time with people who are different from us, and allowing our patterns of thinking to be challenged by diversity and difference. Additionally, it means cultivating the habit of being curious and learning to ask questions from a place of curiosity rather than lapsing into making snap judgments.

The unproductive alternative to this successful resolution is to approach the world with **Deluded Certitude**. Deluded Certitude is born from the unshakable belief in one's convictions without the need to test them against reality. It is an act of hubris and misdirected passion – targeted not at your purpose and values, but instead at maintaining your self-image and pride. Think back to Jason and his unwarranted, unwavering conviction that his work with the Persuasion Marketing would continue unchanged.

Adaptive Impact – The Challenge of Driving Successful Execution

For too long, we have lived with leadership models and images of the superhuman, unrealistic abilities of the leader who has all the answers ready, a strategy at hand, and a team of people assembled and ready to go. That there is a gendered element to this image goes without saying; it is, after all, called the *great man* approach to leadership. This also leads to posturing and gamesmanship; with all the deceptions and shenanigans we have seen too often in supposed leaders.

Adaptive Impact requires a very different orientation: it is about a focus on the tide the leader is guiding and not the leader themselves; it is about delivering results-beyond-results. By results-beyond-results, we mean delivering the immediate targeted results such as key performance indicators (KPIs), objectives & key results (OKRs), adjusted operating income (AOI), and net promoter score (NPS), while simultaneously delivering results in the following three additional areas:

- Followership – Coalescing human energy by creating a direction and a momentum that others will seek to follow.
- Sustainability – Delivering value in a way that outpaces the resources consumed and continually exploring innovative ways of crafting the future.
- Humanocity – Combining the potential of human creativity with the efficiency and speed of automation, creating more than either could individually.

The practice of Adaptive Impact centers around the idea that you can see yourself as the author of the story that is unfolding around you, rather than as a character merely driven along by the plot. However – and this is a big however – the practice of Adaptive Impact requires you to approach the idea of writing your own story with humility, recognizing that the story you write exists within the tide which cannot be controlled – but can be shaped! When we refer to leaders "creating impact," we tend to assume that the action is driven by the leader.

Adaptive impact requires you to disrupt the existing flow by first stepping into the tide to create an ambitious new story for others to follow and to continually resolve the talent challenge to enable the organization to make this new story come to life.

Stepping into the Tide

To guide the tide, you must first step into it. The trick to finding a place to stand is finding a place where your actions are likely to have the maximum impact! Stepping into the tide requires locating the critical pivot point where these complex components meet and then creating meaningful disruption to shape the flow; an action that alters the direction of the flow in an intentionally constructive way.

One way to start is what we call the "Humble Safari," which involves reaching into and learning about your organization beyond your formal accountabilities and seeking to locate the critical pivot point where the complex components of the tide meet and create opportunity. Once you have located these critical pivot points, you need to disrupt the tide by challenging the prevailing group schema. While "group schema" may sound like what is often called "culture," it is much more than that. It is the template that shapes and determines how people think and behave. Challenging this involves surfacing difficult questions and exposing underlying assumptions to be tested and reset, thus, creating a meaningful disruption to shape the flow of the tide.

Embodying Ambitious Realism (and the Power of Inclusive Storytelling)

If stepping into the tide helps disrupt the way those around us think about how the world works, Embodying Ambitious Realism is about taking this disruption forward to shape the way the organization acts. Shaping "the ways of working" – our norms, our culture – is the necessary companion to disrupting the way we think. The key leadership skill or medium to accomplishing this is through inclusive storytelling. More than ever, in an increasingly virtual and physically disconnected world, leaders build connection, engagement, and meaning through stories. They themselves become visible through the stories they tell and prompt others to take authorship of their own stories.

Embodying ambitious realism requires a leader to tell two types of stories. One is a story about what is. Leaders need to create a shared narrative about what the tide looks like right now – that is the "realism" part. The "ambition" part of ambitious realism comes from telling stories about the future, what could be, and what might be possible. These future-oriented stories help to create a shared narrative about how the tide *could* be shifted. They create a common conversation that allows aspiration to become strategy, then policy, and then reality.

That stories can not only shape but create the future has long been acknowledged. As Arthur C. Clarke[9] said, "Any sufficiently advanced technology is indistinguishable from magic." And yet, the magic often becomes reality. The handheld tablets of Star Trek became the iPad, Dick Tracy's wrist-watch TV is now in everyone's pocket. In fact, according to historian Yuval Harari,[10] stories are <u>the</u> power of humanity.

What do future-oriented stories look like? They can take many forms, but the one essential and common element in the stories is that they include the listener. Inclusion in its truest sense is about engaging across a spectrum of views, perspectives, and life experience in a way that brings voices both into the room and, importantly, together.

To summarize: you can create a disruption in the flow of the tide by stepping into it and creating a new inclusive story of what could be; this can dramatically shift the flow and lead to a new way of acting. But this only works if you – and your organization – have the skills and capabilities to execute it.

The Talent Challenge – Maintaining Relevance to the Challenges Ahead

Tackling the talent challenge means ensuring that you and those others around you remain continually relevant to meet the obstacles and seize the new opportunities emerging on the horizon. The focus on building talent must be approached with the same humility as the humble safari; there must be constant, open questioning and at comfort with uncertainty. You can successfully approach the Talent Challenge with what we refer to as Dynamic Curiosity and Curating Capabilities.

Dynamic Curiosity involves helping others and yourself to become comfortable with uncertainty and to remain constantly curious, always asking what different demands the future will impose. Dynamic Curiosity helps you and the organization adapt and move quickly by fostering continuous learning and a willingness to let go of the irrelevant. Addressing future opportunities and obstacles also requires Curating Capabilities. Curating capabilities refer to the ability to constantly scan and compare the demands of the environment to your strengths and those of your team, and to continually refine the list of needed skills – and then doing the work to develop those skills. The goal of Curating Capabilities is to continually ensure relevance and to find paths to combine the potential human and automated work, even at the task level.

A MARIA MOMENT

With a knock on the door, Billy walks into Maria's office. Billy was a fairly new analyst in Maria's department and very ambitious. "Thanks for spending time with me," chirped Bill. "I really want to do well here, and I was hoping I could pick your brain a bit. I want to get some insight into what made you successful so I can plan my own development."

"I appreciate the ambition, Billy," Maria responded, "But I think you're asking the wrong question. What helped me won't help you. You need to be looking forward rather than backwards. Let me suggest this; let's not talk about me. Let's talk about where the business is going. Then go and speak to a few other people and come back in a week or two. Then we can figure out what you need to learn to meet the challenges that are coming up rather than the challenges I faced in the past."

Billy sighed, realizing this was not going to be as simple as putting together a list of "to dos." "Ok," he said, "what's coming down the pike?" Just as she was about to launch into her sense of what the future had in store, Maria took a step back, "I will say one thing about what I think has helped me, you do need to be curious, about everything."

What Is the Challenge that Must Be Resolved in Adaptive Impact

The alternative to Adaptive Impact is for leaders to become **Stuck in Neutral**. Leaders who are Stuck in Neutral lead their teams and organizations to continually deliver the same outcomes, making modest, continual, incremental improvements, and eventually costing the organization more (either in direct revenue loss or through opportunity costs) than they deliver. Stuck in Neutral is a state in which we not only fail to address challenges but we eventually fall into a position in which we ignore those challenges for the sake of comfort and continuity, becoming comfortably numb to what's going on around us.

We have looked at the details of our three practices for guiding the tide. In each case, we discussed the critical capabilities and the traps to avoid.

What we haven't discussed is how you can develop these practices. Let's turn to that challenge now.

How Do Leaders Evolve? – Mindsets, Vertical Growth, and Turns

As the image of Frida Kahlo reminded Maria Miller, she had once faced challenges similar to what Jason was facing – and she had failed. In examining her failure, Maria drew productive lessons about how she could grow as a leader.

Much work has already been done in the field of leadership development and we can use that work as a springboard to help us understand how leaders like Maria (and ourselves) evolve. Harvard Professor Bob Kegan's[11] work on leadership development speaks to the importance of evolving by shifting your mindset through various developmental stages, thereby expanding your ways of thinking. Critical to this evolution is the idea of evolving the way we think – from seeing individual items or actions, to seeing these individuals or actions as part of a category (pattern recognition), and then to seeing categories as part of an integrated system that reflects and reacts within itself (systems thinking).

Nicholas Petri[12] at the Center for Creative Leadership took this concept a step further and provided a compelling concept of bi-directional growth in leaders. He referred to vertical growth as shifting mindsets while horizontal growth occurred through the expansion of capabilities, competencies, and experiences. We see this as a crucial concept: a person's capacity to lead lives at the interaction between their mindset and what we refer to as their behavioral range – the set of capabilities, competencies, and experiences they have to draw upon (Figure 2.2).

While these fundamental concepts provide a clearer understanding of *what* leadership development looks like, they still do not help us understand *how* leadership development actually happens. The how of leadership development is better understood through a stepped journey. Metaphors like these abound in leadership development literature including "Passages," "Seasons," "Stages of Maturity," or "Turns" – all based on the observation that leadership growth is not a straight line. It is an ongoing iterative process, constantly being shaped by meaningful, impactful experiences. These moments in our lives stand out because their sharp edges and jagged points press us to examine our assumptions, beliefs, and

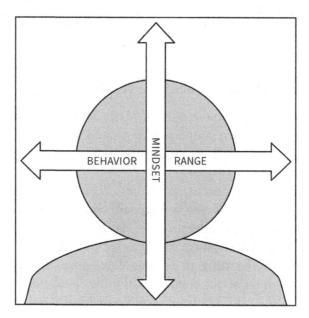

FIGURE 2.2
Capacity to Lead

behaviors. We will dig into the how of leadership development more deeply in Chapter 7.

A MARIA MOMENT

On arriving in London, prior to joining Percipience Ltd., Maria worked for a large multi-media publishing company in a finance service center leading the accounts payable process for the business. Her team handled tens of thousands of transactions involving multiple billions of dollars annually. After a few years, Maria was being considered for a critical regional commercial leadership role and so she participated in a high-pressure simulation experience modeling this potential role. She failed so badly that the assessment was ended prematurely. The experience was life changing. Maria described her career at the publishing house up to that point as looking through a window covered with blinds – not realizing what the business was truly about. For her, after the experience with the simulation, it was as if the blinds had been stripped away and her view had dramatically expanded. Maria went on to take a role

> *on the commercial side of the business that was, organizationally, a step back but that provided a platform for learning. Eighteen months later, she was ready for and received the leadership role she originally sought.*

As Aldous Huxley famously said, *"Experience is not so much what happens to a man; it is what a man does with what happens with him."* Developing the capacity to guide the tide requires you to recognize and capitalize on critical moments of experience and to mine these moments for learning. To do that requires understanding the mindset and capabilities that go into each of the three practices of Honest Engagement, Addressing Reality, and Adaptive Impact.

IN SUMMARY

In this chapter, we have tried to summarize what it means to approach leadership with agency and, in so doing, guide the tide of events around you. We have introduced several new key concepts. They are summarized in Figure 2.3.

Throughout the remainder of this book, we will delve more deeply into each of the three practices we have outlined in this chapter. In doing so, we will introduce some new ideas and will include a similar table summarizing those key concepts. Also, just as we begin each chapter with another peek into the story of Maria Miller, we will conclude with a few words to wrap up her story. Here is wrap-up of this chapter's story:

On her drive home that evening after letting Jason go, Maria Miller's thoughts turned to her lost promotion back in 2008. "Wow, that really hurt," she said out loud to no one. "And running away to London, well, it turned out ok, but it probably wasn't the best response."

"Did it matter where you were?" asked Frida Kahlo whose image appeared to Maria in the passenger seat.

"No, not really," said Maria. "What really mattered was that I learned something. It hurt, but I needed to take stock of what had happened and try to make some sense out it to change the way I approached the world."

"I hope Jason learns something from all of this," Maria said as she pulled into her driveway and the image of Frida faded away.

GUIDING THE TIDE A leader's capacity to realistically and productively engage with "The Tide" to deliver results-beyond-results.	
CONCEPT SUMMARY	
The Tide	The unique but ever-changing stream of systems, technology, society, consumers, and competitors powered by human energy within the larger ocean of economic, social, political, physical, and environmental forces.
Results-Beyond-Results	Critical outcomes beyond the achievement of specific business targets: followership, sustainability, and humanocity.
Followership	Coalescing human energy by creating a direction and momentum that others seek to follow, goals that others adopt, and a vision that others share.
Sustainability	Driving renewable value by creating value in a way that outpaces the resources consumed, and continually exploring innovative ways of crafting the future.
Humanizing	Integrating human creativity with technological efficiency by creating meaning for individuals and communities.
Honest Engagement	Dealing with others from a place of openness, honesty, and a willingness to be vulnerable.
Addressing Reality	Seeing the world as it is rather than as we wish it to be; the ability to separate fact from fiction and data from desire.
Adaptive Impact	Leading the organization, team, and one's self forward in a way that creates sustainable success and on-going relevance by stepping into the tide, embodying ambitious realism and meeting the talent challenge.

FIGURE 2.3
Guiding the Tide Concept Summary

NOTES

1 Bob Johansen, *The New Leadership Literacies: Thriving in a Future of Extreme Disruption and Distributed Everything*, First edition (Oakland, California: BK, Berrett-Koehler Publishers, Inc., 2017).

2 Ronald A, Alexander Grashow, and Marty Linsky, *The Practice of Adaptive Leadership: Tools and Tactics for Changing Your Organization and the World* (Boston, Mass: Harvard Business Press, 2009).

3 Joseph Campbell and Robert Walter, *A Joseph Campbell Companion: Reflections on the Art of Living* (Csorna: Joseph Campbell Foundation, 2017).

4 Sudhanshu Palsule and Michael Chavez, *Rehumanizing Leadership: Putting Purpose Back into Business* (Madrid: LID, 2020).

5 Milton Rokeach, *The Nature of Human Values* (New York: Free Press, 1973).

6 Charles A. O'Reilly and Jeffrey Pfeffer, "Why Are Grandiose Narcissists More Effective at Organizational Politics? Means, Motive, and Opportunity," *Personality and Individual Differences* 172 (April 2021): 110557, https://doi.org/10.1016/j.paid.2020.110557.

7 Herminia Ibarra, *Act like a Leader, Think like a Leader* (Boston, Mass: Harvard Business Review Press, 2015).

8 Alfred Korzybski, *Science and Sanity: An Introduction to Non-Aristotelian Systems and General Semantics*, 5th Ed., 3rd print (Brooklyn, NY: Inst. of General Semantics, 2005).

9 Arthur C. Clarke. *Profiles of the Future: An Inquiry into the Limits of the Possible*. 3rd Rev. Ed. (New York: Grand Central Publishing 1985).

10 Harari, Y. N, Sapiens: A brief history of humankind (First U.S. edition). (New York: Harper, 2015).

11 Robert Kegan, *In over Our Heads: The Mental Demands of Modern Life*, 4th print (Cambridge, Mass.: Harvard Univ. Press, 1997).

12 Nick Petrie, "Vertical Leadership Development – Part 1: Developing Leaders for a Complex World," White Paper (Greensboro, NC: Center for Creative Leadership, November 2014), https://mdvconsulting.co/wp-content/uploads/CCL-VerticalLeadersPart1.pdf (p.14).

3

Honest Engagement

The challenge of understanding yourself and relating to others from a place of openness, honesty, and a willingness to be vulnerable, rather than presenting a transactional façade (Figure 3.1).

  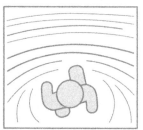

HONEST ENGAGEMENT	**ADDRESSING REALITY**	**ADAPTIVE IMPACT**
Purpose	Seeking & Interpreting Information	Stepping into the Tide
Values	Enrolling Others	Ambitious Realism
Empathy	Maintaining Mindfulness	Managing the Talent Challenge

FIGURE 3.1
Guiding the Tide Practices: Honest Engagement

DOI: 10.4324/9781003491880-3

WHERE MARIA LEARNS TO PAY ATTENTION TO HERSELF

Life at Percipience Ltd. was never dull, *thought Maria to herself as she started packing her things at 7:30 on a Friday evening. The afternoon had passed by in a blur and she was already late for a long overdue catch-up at her favorite bar with her colleagues Bill and Ajay. The morning had begun uneventfully.* "Why can't all Fridays be like this?" *she had remarked at the end of the third meeting. Precisely ten minutes later, her boss, Simon, walked in and sat down opposite her.* "I've just come out of the Management Committee meeting," *he began with a grave look on his face.* "They've stretched our target by another 5%, and we need to make those numbers quickly." *Before Maria could respond, he smiled and said,* "I'm really counting on you, Maria. If anyone can make this happen, it's you." *Maria was in a daze as Simon left the room. The timing couldn't have been worse. The Management Committee could have just left it to the next quarter, she thought to herself. Her team had worked hard, very hard, and it was not going to be easy to have this conversation with them. Maria needed a coffee.*

While waiting for her espresso at the cafeteria, Maria checked her phone and saw she had three missed calls from Leon, the global head of marketing at Clearwater Biotech. Leon was a customer who had become a friend. She walked to a quiet table and called him back. "Where have you been, Maria, I've been trying to get you since the morning!" *he said when he answered. Cutting short Maria's apology, he spoke animatedly,* "Listen, I've got a great opportunity for you, and I haven't reached out to anyone else. I'm sending you all the details by email now, but lemme just tell you, this could be worth a lot." *Maria hurried back to her office, taken aback at the turn of events. First, a shocker from her boss, and then, as if on cue, seemingly divine intervention!*

Maria canceled her next two meetings and went through Leon's proposal. Clearwater had been conducting trials for a new drug and there were strong indications it would be a success. After scanning the global information marketplace, Leon's company had located and purchased a massive database from which they needed to identify and distill consumer insights, so they could begin a targeted social media marketing campaign as soon as possible. They needed Percipience Ltd. as a partner to supply the technology and the "smarts," as Leon called it, to succeed. The FDA was likely to approve the drug in the next six months and Clearwater wanted to be ready to hit the ground running with the marketing campaign.

Despite her exhilaration at this incredible opportunity, Maria felt strangely discomforted. Something was bothering her, and she couldn't quite put her finger on it. She rang two trusted team members, Mark and Jenny, and asked them for an urgent meeting. Once they had read through the proposal, Maria asked, "So, what's your assessment?"

Mark cleared his throat and said, "Well … so many other companies are doing this, so why shouldn't we?"

"Doing what? What are you talking about?" asked Maria.

Now it was Jenny's turn to speak: "Well, you know we're going to be tapping into personal data without the explicit consent of those whose data it is. There's nothing illegal about it, that's just the way everything works nowadays. It's part of the new consumer rules of engagement in the digital age!"

Maria thanked them both. It was almost seven and she wanted to get that drink with Bill and Ajay. But just as she was leaving the office, her phone rang again. It was her boss. "I've just had a call from the Clearwater folks, I was told Leon had reached out to you?" While Maria was trying to compose her reply, he continued, "Maria, this is a big deal; let's nail it."

One gin and tonic later, Maria found herself sharing her thoughts with Bill and Ajay. Ajay laughed away her concerns and said, "Business is business, Maria." Bill was a bit more circumspect, and he advised Maria to sleep on it.

All through Saturday, Maria kept going back and forth in her thoughts, confused and unsure. She woke up early on Sunday morning and went for a long walk in the woods. After an hour, Maria stopped by a stream and found a place to sit down among the stones and trees. As she closed her eyes, she imagined Frida Kahlo sitting next to her. "Why is this decision so troubling, Frida?" she asked her imaginary friend and muse.

"No one can help you out of this one, Maria," Frida replied. "You already have the answer inside you, but you don't have the confidence to face it." Frida's face was serious. "Maria, to do the right thing, we need to be guided by some inner compass, a feeling that speaks to you…", Frida said as she trailed off.

"But what if I don't know what I feel?" asked Maria.

Frida considered before answering. She looked straight into Maria's eyes and said, "You have never paid much attention to these things before, never given it a shape or form. Look back at your life and ask yourself, what has always mattered to you? Explore those moments when you have felt the resonance of rightness, and those when you have not. Connect the dots, Maria, and you will be able to recognize what your life is meant to be about. And once you know what it is, you will find the courage to live it." Frida paused for a moment and said, "It's very pretty here," as she faded from Maria's mind.

Maria walked back home with a lightness in her step. She had no idea what she was going to do, but she was certain it was going to be okay.

In the story above, Maria is grappling with a deep dilemma which touched her both personally and professionally. Dilemmas are different from problems in that they do not have any one clear, objective solution, and often the only way to resolve them is to allow your purpose and values to guide you into making the right choices and taking the actions that support those choices. When asked to explain the difference between those who manage and those who lead, Warren Bennis[1] wisely said, "Managers do things right while leaders do the right thing." But what precipitates the right action? And for whom is the action right – the one who must decide and take the action, or the ones who are affected by the action? Sometimes, the right action brings challenges in its wake and choosing to take such an action may seem like the more difficult choice. However, rather than looking at it as a choice, the right action can be seen as a result – a consequence – of what we call Honest Engagement.

HONEST ENGAGEMENT – NAVIGATING LEADERSHIP DILEMMAS

Honest Engagement means dealing with others from a place of openness, honesty, and a willingness to be vulnerable. While this has always been an important implied feature of productive leadership, we feel that it must become an explicit, fundamental ability for leaders who need to navigate in a complex, fast-moving, and disruptive 21st century in which there are no easy answers from playbooks. Honest Engagement is what enables leaders to become role models, creating trust, and helping to unite others around goals that really matter. Honest Engagement is at the heart of the concept of *Guiding the Tide*.

As we stressed in the opening chapters of this book, the critical outcome of building leadership agency to "guide the tide" is to deliver results-beyond-results. That is, not only delivering the critical immediate targets and goals you seek, but to do so in a way that builds: followership, sustainability, and Humanocity within your organization. As we go forward, we will summarize the outcomes in each of these areas delivered by each Guiding the Tide practice and the critical skills necessary to deliver them.

Honest Engagement: Dealing with others from a place of openness, honesty, and a willingness to be vulnerable.		
FOLLOWERSHIP	SUSTAINABILITY	HUMANOCITY
Outcome: Creating trust	**Outcome:** Coalescing energy around the goals that matter	**Outcome:** Leader as a role model
Skills: Using purpose as a driver of authentic conversations	**Skills:** Unearthing core values to guide actions and decisions	**Skills:** Using empathy as the path to engage others

FIGURE 3.2
Honest Engagement

The chart above summarizes the outcomes that Honest Engagement creates in each of these areas as well as the skills discussed in this chapter that are needed to drive these outcomes (Figure 3.2).

The Two Sides of Honest Engagement – Looking Inside-Out and Outside-In

There are two dimensions to Honest Engagement. One is the ability to engage with the very core of yourself, serving as an *inside-out* compass to navigate in the external world. The other dimension is the ability to engage with an *outside-in* perspective, which guides your perceptions and actions. While the former answers the question, "*What must I do?*" the latter answers the question, "*What am I being called upon to do?*"

Both perspectives are important in responding to leadership dilemmas. Think of the first perspective, "What must I do?" as an *autobiographical* perspective; it is the story we tell about ourselves – to ourselves and to others. Think of the second perspective, "What am I being called upon to do?" as a *biographical* one. It is the story others tell about us, what they say to each other about us when we are not in the room. When the two perspectives work together, they balance each other and intersect to create a more truthful and authentic foundation for how you show up as a leader (Figure 3.3).

As executive coaches and consultants we have worked with many leaders who get lost when one of those two perspectives goes missing or the

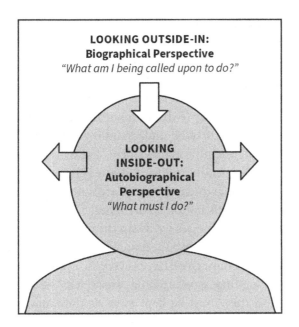

FIGURE 3.3
The Dilemma of Honest Engagement

autobiographical and biographical perspectives are misaligned. When the biographical perspective gets lost, the autobiographical perspective can become delusional or narcissistic. When you are guided by the biographical perspective alone without the balance of the inside-out perspective, you can turn into a leader with no anchor, a political creature with the singular intention of staying afloat.

The Autobiographical Perspective – What Must I Do?

What happened to Maria reflects what all of us must go through in our development as human beings and as leaders. Often called "a moment of truth," this is when you must simultaneously confront both the world and yourself and draw upon the inner resources you carry deep within to point you in the direction you must take. The problem for many of us is that these inner resources – *our core values and our purpose* – are often underdeveloped, unclear, and are sometimes practically invisible. While many of us devote considerable time and effort to honing other critical resources such as analytical skills, the ability to debate and argue a point, the capacity to break down a problem into its constituent parts, and the ability to understand detail, we do not always devote the effort to developing the equally critical resources of values and purpose.

Although it sounds straightforward, guiding yourself by values and purpose – our deepest feelings – is hard. There are various reasons for this. On the one hand, an inability to draw on our feelings is a consequence of a long-standing cultural bias of understanding ourselves as "thinking beings." A century of "scientific management" has driven home the notion that what really matters in life and work is our ability to analyze and dissect. The rest – the feelings and emotions – are nothing but an appendage, and a nuisance at that. This notion is further exacerbated by the countless tools, frameworks, and processes we use in the pursuit of what we assume is a rational way of doing things. We assume that clear thinking must be devoid of anything but objective data, as everything else just ends up adding vagueness or clouding issues. Feelings are seen as the worst culprits in this narrative, and they must be kept away as they muddy the waters. Trekkies will know what we mean when we say that our ideal world has been the purview of Spock: one in which analytical thought devoid of emotion is king. Even though such a notion has been disproved by advances in medical science, which demonstrate that emotion is an integral part of the thinking process,[2] it has remained a cultural myth that still endures, particularly in the leadership and business worlds.

The second reason for the difficulty around being in touch with one's feelings is that we are simply not trained to do so. The dominant cultural myth outlined above has also resulted in the absence of an educational or a developmental process geared toward understanding who we are on an emotional level. Most of us stumble into the need to understand our values and purpose during our lives, or on a rare, thoughtful leadership development program. When Frida asked Maria to find out what she was feeling, she was asking her to explore nothing less than her fundamental response to the world. A feeling is a response to a stimulus, just like analytic thought. Without having taken the time to develop an understanding of your purpose and values, you likely do not have the ability to notice what your feelings are telling you, or worse still, you may hear the voice, but choose to ignore it.

Honest Engagement, dealing with others from a place of openness, honesty, and a willingness to be vulnerable, begins by developing the ability to use your core values and purpose as a guide to action. Pete Carroll, the great American football coach who led the University of Southern California from 2001 to 2009 and the Seattle Seahawks of the NFL from 2010 to 2023 had this to say on the subject,

> *To me, the essence of being as good as you can be is you have to figure out who you are. You have to figure out that and (give) relentless effort to try and get clear about what's important to you, what uncompromising principles do you stand by, what makes you who you are. If you don't go through that process, you don't do that self-discovery, you don't have an opportunity to be your best because you don't know who you are yet.*[3]

This is the foundation of the autobiographical perspective. Let's explore each in turn.

Core Values

Core values reflect both what you value in others and what makes you feel valued. Your core values are a judgment that some outcomes or some approaches have more worth than others. Core values are hard to identify. When you get your team together and ask them to talk about their values, the usual suspects crop up: integrity, trust, honesty, team spirit, etc. But are these *really* your core values or simply what we have learned to call our values? Core values are deeply emotional – they are felt, not thought. They are most clearly understood when you begin looking at the patterns in your life experiences and determining what really matters to you.

When you actually live out your core values, you may not notice them at all. It is typically when they are challenged, or when you find yourself behaving in ways that are antithetical to your values, that the disquiet begins. This disquiet is the cost of engaging others through a *transactional façade*, continually shifting the values you show to others to match the demands of the moment rather than your true core values. The disquiet may start off as a feeble voice trying to be heard against the din of all the other thoughts and feelings, but if unheeded, it soon becomes a cry for help. The more you ignore that value call, the more havoc it creates.

That havoc may appear as a state of distraction, as we use constant motion to create noise to drown out the inner cry so that we are able to pay attention to our own values. The havoc can also appear as severe stress, the consequence of the conflict between your deepest feelings about what you must do, and what you actually end up doing. And most certainly, this havoc can appear as, and result in, a diminished level of trust between yourself and those you try to lead, as your actions seem unpredictable and untethered to your true selves.

So how do you become more aware of your core values and consistently align your decisions and actions to your values? As Darden Professor Mary Gentile conveys in her landmark book,[4] most of us already want to act on our values and give them voice by overcoming the biases and constraints from our lived experiences, cultural norms, and social contexts. Gentile makes the case that the ability to connect to your core values and "giving voice" to them can guide leaders to their best actions and outcomes. Like a muscle that can be trained through practice, you can build this capability by continually focusing on the questions: "What would it look like if I acted on my values?" and "What would I say and do?"

The trick is to learn to listen to your body and your feelings to pick up the early signals: the pain-signal of values being trampled, and the joy-signal of your values being lived. To truly begin to discover your core values, look back on critical dilemmas in your life, moments when the demands of the moment were in conflict with your inner demands. Ask yourself, *"When did I act on my values, what did I do and say?"* Look for patterns to uncover the core values you truly hold.

Purpose

Values are judgments about the relative worth of outcomes and approaches, and core values are those values that hold the highest personal worth. Purpose, on the other hand, is a point of view on the fundamental question – why do we exist? Don't panic – we do not pose this question in the broad, theological sense of the reason for human existence. Rather, purpose is a targeted, focused question addressing the role of this organization, this department, this group, myself in this place and time. Purpose answers the questions: *"What is the unique contribution I wish to make and how do I make our world a better place?"*[5]

Daniel Pink[6] helpfully breaks purpose down into two concepts: the first is purpose in the sense of *"How am I making a difference?"* This attributes a broader meaning to purpose that transcends a particular circumstance and speaks to how we strive to have the work of our organization, department, or ourselves as a whole, impact our larger ecosystem. The second concept is purpose as the contribution we make to the endeavors of a larger group to which we feel connected: *"How do I contribute to the work of my team; how does my department contribute to the success of the enterprise (and the world?)"*

Understanding purpose from both of these perspectives is critical – (1) what impact do I (and those I lead) strive to make on my larger ecosystem? and (2) what contribution do I (and those I lead) make to the success of the larger enterprise we care about? Impact and contribution: these are the essence of purpose.

A MARIA MOMENT

It was Sunday evening and Maria was sitting in her favorite reclining chair by the window, composing her thoughts about what she was going to tell her boss the next morning. Her mind was calm, which surprised her as this was unusual for a Sunday evening. She found her thoughts drifting to her chance meeting with Nancy, the founder of Percipience Ltd., who had now become a non-exec on the Board, at a corporate event four years ago. Maria sought out Nancy in the crowd and engaged her in conversation. What struck Maria was Nancy's passion and clarity, and the way she described her reasons for creating the company. "Business is about finding ways of helping people's lives in one way or the other," she had said. "Percipience Ltd. is more than just a data company: our purpose is to use information to improve the lives of people and the societies in which they live." Maria remembered that, after that event and discussion, she had returned home feeling good about being at Percipience Ltd. It had been four years and she hadn't thought about this meeting with Nancy until now.

"Finding" Purpose

Crafting a sense of your purpose – both the impact you wish to have and the contribution you wish to make – can be deeply challenging, as it is as much an emotional effort as it is an intellectual one (Figure 3.4). One way to approach this journey is to think of purpose as being located at the intersection of the following four questions:[7]

1. What are the themes that stand out in your life story? (Passion)
2. What are you really good at? (Skills and abilities)
3. What do you most profoundly care about? (Contribution)
4. What does your team or organization need to deliver? (Impact)

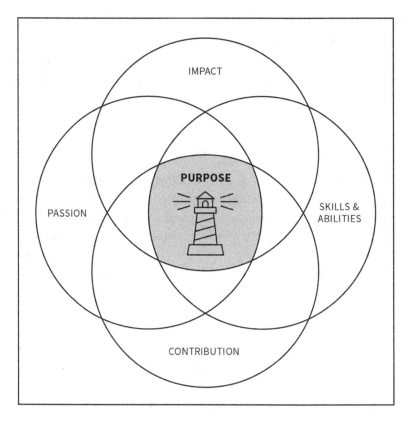

FIGURE 3.4
Understanding Purpose

Finding purpose is like an excavation project in that you need to dig deep within yourself to uncover what lays at your foundation.

Begin by identifying your personal narrative – your story. What are you passionate about? How do you explain yourself to others? What has driven you forward in life?

Second, honestly assess what you are good at. What are your unique skills and abilities?

Third, identify what you truly care about. This is difficult as the list can be long. Be ruthless in your choices. To what are you really willing to commit yourself?

And finally, what are the aspirations of your organization – and what is most needed to obtain them? The common thread across all of these questions is precisely where you will begin to unearth purpose – the impact and contribution that you consistently strive to make.

The impact and contribution are authentically yours. Authenticity, as the Canadian psychiatrist Gabor Maté[8] describes it, is the ability to be in touch with our deepest feelings and allowing them to become a guide for action. The purpose, then, is the fulcrum of authenticity, the lever that allows us to be true to ourselves and anchored in meaning, without which we are tossed around by the flow of the tide rather than anchored and guiding it. This is where we find the balance between humility and ego. Humility is critical as it allows us to find value in others and the wider world. Leading with agency means seeing value in your own purpose and having the inner strength to bring this purpose forward.

The Biographical Perspective – What Am I Being Called upon to Do?

In contrast to the autobiographical view, the biographical perspective is being able to observe a situation and your response to it from an outside-in view. This allows you to sharpen your awareness of your values and purpose and to explore how they can be utilized in service to the world. If Honest Engagement is limited to your autobiographical view – considering only your values and purpose in relationship to yourself – you run the risk of engaging in leadership that is self-serving and narcissistic.

Short-term versus long-term; narrow versus broad; immediate profits versus sustainable profits: these are real dilemmas that most leaders must confront in the course of their careers. Rosabeth Moss Kanter[9] has an expression for this: she used the terms "economic logic" and "institutional logic" to describe this dilemma. As Kanter describes it, economic logic is necessary for delivering sustainable economic returns above the cost of capital, that is, delivering on immediate objectives. Institutional logic is the ability to sustain the conditions (in society and with people) that allow you to flourish over time, in our words, delivering results-beyond-results. We often ignore the institutional logic, focusing instead on maximizing short-term gain – or economic logic – which is a lot more tangible and easier to measure.

How do we find our way past these dilemmas? Focusing on our core values and purpose is certainly a way forward. However, untethered to the needs of the ecosystem surrounding us, we can be tempted to choose actions that are only right for ourselves without considering if they are right for others. To balance values and purpose with the "greater good" requires the widest span of empathy.

Finding Empathy

Geoff Colvin[10] describes empathy as "understanding the feelings of others and reacting in an appropriate manner." Thus, he suggests empathy has both an emotional and behavioral component. Paul Bloom[11] (among others) has demonstrated that the emotional and behavioral aspects of empathy are insufficient without being directed by reason – a cognitive component must be added to the emotional and behavioral components of empathy.

What is the path to finding empathy – a positive, productive, emotional, cognitive, and behavioral response to others? In other words, how can you understand what a situation or person calls upon you to do? Many years ago, psychologist Erich Fromm[12] looked at a similar question and came up with a three-part strategy, addressing these three areas. He believed for us to truly connect with those around us we need to:

1. Know them
2. Understand them
3. Care about them

Let's look at these in turn. Knowing someone is the rational aspect of empathy. You need to take the time to learn about their goals, agendas, challenges, and capabilities. Understanding someone is the emotional aspect of empathy. It is about learning their values and purpose with openness and without judgment. In other words, it is the ability to be able to "feel where they are coming from." Caring about someone is the behavioral aspect of empathy. It is a willingness to engage in efforts – to act and make decisions – to help them further their values and purpose within the context of their goals, agendas, and constraints. This same approach can be extended to other groups, other organizations, etc.

Honest Engagement – Balancing the Inside-Out and Outside-In Perspectives

When you take the two perspectives together – the autobiographical and the biographical – they provide the vantage point of Honest

Engagement, however complex and ambiguous the situation may be. The danger zone of complexity and ambiguity is always inertia, the pressure to stand still while the overwhelming nature of the events of the world unfold. As we have repeatedly stressed, leadership agency is the ability to step forward into the tide of events, and to bring others along with you. Any step forward requires firm footing. Honest Engagement provides that footing.

First, Honest Engagement can serve as an inside-out anchor to guide your actions based on a clear understanding of your core values and purpose. However, be warned, seeking your core values and purpose in the midst of action is very difficult. Take the time to exercise these muscles continually, being sure that you hone these self-insights as you would any other capability. That way, when the time comes to make a decision about what best serves your core values and purpose, you will be well-practiced, having already done the necessary self-reflection. Second, the outside-in guidepost provided by empathy clarifies the potential impacts your actions can have and allows you to balance "what you must do" to be true to yourself with "what you are called to do" to be of positive service to those around you.

Ignoring the practice of Honest Engagement leads to an alternative response which we have referred to as *Transactional Façade*. This is a state where an individual portrays a false front – a façade – to those around them. Not only is this front false disconnected from your true values and purpose, but it is ever-shifting. The front "face" we end up showing others is based on our perception of what the circumstances call for to achieve immediate, short-term success or to avoid immediate, short-term pain. It is a transaction – *I will be who you want me to be if it lets me move forward in the moment.* This is the best way to destroy trust.

Alternatively, Honest Engagement builds trust as it creates a level of predictability. Those you seek to lead will learn about your values and your purpose and consequently will have insight into your thinking and reactions. Further, as they come to expect you to show empathy, they will build comfort in approaching you honestly as well. While most of the work of Honest Engagement takes place within yourself, its most visible expression is in how it prompts your ability to have Authentic Conversations with others. This can begin a virtuous cycle in which others are encouraged to hold Authentic Conversations themselves.

Authentic Conversations

An authentic conversation has three elements to it:

1. It is a **con**versation, the prefix "con" indicating that it is together with another. It is not about telling but engaging in a meaningful dialogue.
2. It involves an honest disclosure of your feelings and assumptions in a way that nudges the other to do the same.
3. It is much more about context than about content. Context means, "to weave together" both your own and the other person's intended perspectives so that the other person finds value and meaning in the discussion.

Authentic conversations are difficult because they involve your having to endure the double discomfort of entering the knotty domain of expressing feelings, and being unsure of the outcome. In Maria's case, this discomfort was further amplified by the fact that she needed to have an authentic conversation with her boss, Simon. For those of you who have been in that situation before, you know the pressure she was feeling.

Authentic conversations need preparation of two kinds. One, they require you to be in a calm and composed state of mind in which you feel the warmth of quiet confidence. There is a sense of being anchored in yourself and being true to who you are in those moments that begins to permeate every part of you.

The other prep is the kind that athletes engage in before a match or game, or actors before a performance – the dress rehearsal before the actual performance. In this case, the dress rehearsal involves constructing the narrative of the conversation in your mind. Preparation for an authentic conversation involves thinking through how you will express the three elements of Honest Engagement, balancing the inside-out and outside-in:

- How will I portray my *purpose* in a way that is true to what I believe, and connects with the way this audience understands the world so that I can help us find a common purpose?
- How will I convey my *values* in a way that shows I understand the goals and constraints the audience faces so that we can come to the same priorities?
- How will I recommend *action* that furthers my ambitions as well as my audience's ambitions – turning them into joint ambitions?

IN SUMMARY

We began this chapter with an introduction to the practice of Honest Engagement, the foundation of the ability to step into and guide the tide with a sense of agency. Looking into yourself, understanding who you are, and finding a way to balance the story you tell about yourself with the stories others tell about you is a profound, difficult, and dare we say it, personal journey, into yourself. But the resulting outcomes can be extraordinary. When you demonstrate a willingness to be open and vulnerable through sharing your values, you help others around you do the same, thereby forging a shared purpose.

Below are the key concepts we discussed in this chapter (Figure 3.5).

HONEST ENGAGEMENT Dealing with others from a place of openness, honesty, and a willingness to be vulnerable.	
CONCEPT SUMMARY	
Autobiographical Perspective	The story we tell about ourselves, an *inside-out* compass to navigate in the external world, answering the question: "What must I do?"
Biographical Perspective	The story others tell about us, an *outside-in* perspective which guides one's perceptions and actions, answering the question: "What am I called to do?"
Purpose	A targeted, focused understanding of the role of one's organization, department, group, or self, in this place and time consistent with our belief in what we can bring into being over the course of time.
Core Values	Judgments that we hold either of the desirability of an end state or the appropriateness of a way of achieving a goal.
Empathy	A positive, productive emotional, cognitive, and behavioural response to others.
Transactional Façade	An approach in which a leader regularly shifts how they see themselves in order to meet the demands of the moment, matching their actions to what they think others desire.

FIGURE 3.5
Honest Engagement Concept Summary

As thoughts of meeting one of Percipience Ltd.'s founders, Nancy, faded from Maria's mind, an old memory of time with her father came flooding back. She was 20 and had come home for the weekend. She had spoken to her father on the phone just a week before and he had told her that he wanted to meet and go for a long walk. "Long walks" were her father's way of saying he wanted to talk about something important. As they came upon a clearing and stood at the edge of a valley, he looked at her and said, "Maria, you are going to be flying high, and may you soar to great achievements ... but remember one thing: the most precious resource you carry with you on your journey is knowing who you are. Stay close to that essence and never relinquish it."

NOTES

1 Warren G. Bennis, *On Becoming a Leader*, 20th anniversary ed. (New York: Basic Books, 2009).

2 Antonio Damasio, *The Feeling of What Happens: Body and Emotion in the Making of Consciousness* (New York: Harcourt Brace & Company, 1999).

3 Michael-Shawn Dugar, "The Pete Carroll Era Is Over: Here's Why the Seahawks Moved On after 14 Years." *The Athletic* Jan. 11 2014. https://theathletic.com/5194305/2024/01/11/pete-carroll-seahawks-coach-out/.

4 Mary C. Gentile, *Giving Voice to Values: How to Speak Your Mind When You Know What's Right* (New Haven, Conn.: Yale University Press, 2012).

5 Sudhanshu Palsule and Michael Chavez. *Rehumanizing Leadership: Putting Purpose Back into Business* (Madrid: LID, 2020).

6 Daniel H. Pink, *Drive: The Surprising Truth about What Motivates Us*. Reprint, paperback ed . (New York: Riverhead Books, 2012).

7 Adapted from Palsule and Chavez, Rehumanizing *Leadership*.

8 Gabor Maté, *The Myth of Normal: Trauma, Illness and Healing in a Toxic Culture* (London: Vermilion. 2022).

9 Rosabeth Moss Kanter, "How Great Companies Think Differently." *Harvard Business Review* (Nov. 2011).

10 Geoffrey Colvin, *Humans Are Underrated: What High Achievers Know That Brilliant Machines Never Will*, Paperback ed. (New York Portfolio Penguin, 2016).

11 Paul Bloom. *Against Empathy: The Case for Rational Compassion*, First ed. (New York: Ecco, an imprint of HarperCollins Publishers, 2016).

12 Erich Fromm, *The Art of Loving*, 50th anniversary ed., Harper Perennial Modern classics ed. (New York: Harper Perennial, 2006).

4

Addressing Reality

The challenge of perceiving the world as it is rather than how we wish it to be; to separate fact from fiction, data from desire – permitting a focus on what is truly of value (Figure 4.1).

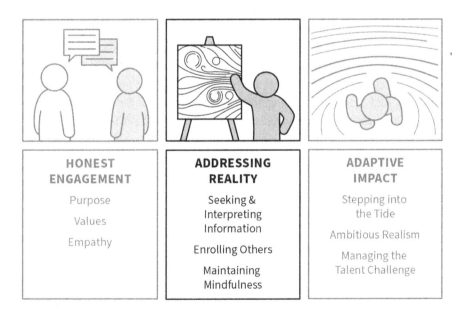

HONEST ENGAGEMENT	ADDRESSING REALITY	ADAPTIVE IMPACT
Purpose	Seeking & Interpreting Information	Stepping into the Tide
Values		Ambitious Realism
Empathy	Enrolling Others	Managing the Talent Challenge
	Maintaining Mindfulness	

FIGURE 4.1
Guiding the Tide Practices: Addressing Reality

DOI: 10.4324/9781003491880-4

WHERE MARIA LEARNS THE DANGER OF BUILDING CASTLES

Some calls are easy, *thought Maria Miller, slightly disappointed as she clicked a PowerPoint shut.* I can't imagine why the team brought us this one.

"Hey Maria," *Joe Robertson, Percipience Ltd.'s CFO said as he popped his head into Maria's office.* "I reviewed the meeting materials, I think we can make this a short one."

"Yeah, sorry about this. Sometimes the team gets excited about an idea without really thinking it through," *Maria replied as she walked Joe to the conference room where the monthly Target Opportunities review meeting was about to start.*

Maria Miller's New Business team was responsible for identifying opportunities to bring to Percipience Ltd. Sometimes these were new market or channel opportunities. More often they were partnerships or acquisition targets that could enhance or expand the reach of a Percipience Ltd. product. Each month the team presented to a senior management committee including Maria, Joe, and Chelsea Lupo, the head of R&D.

The team normally pre-pitched Maria on any new opportunities they were going to bring forward and almost never pitched an idea she rejected. Today was an exception. The team was pitching an idea for a partnership with a firm that had developed management control software for commercial 3D printing applications. They had pitched Maria this idea six weeks ago and it led to a spirited discussion. Maria asked for more time to consider the idea.

Percipience Ltd. had some experience in 3D printing. Five years prior, the firm was brought in to develop software to help create printing designs. After a large initial investment, the effort barely broke even. It turned out that 3D printing, while continuing to be promising, was still a niche technology used in a very limited number of production applications. Now the team was bringing Maria an idea that wasn't even tied directly to the production of 3D printed product components, but one step removed – process management software.

Not wanting to dismiss the idea out of hand, Maria took some time to investigate on her own. She reached out to several colleagues to get their perspective on the growth of 3D printing. She called two key clients who were using 3D printed products to ask about plans to expand the use of these products, discuss the types of challenges they were having, and how Percipience Ltd. might help. Lastly, she called the analyst in the strategy group who had helped with the 3D printing deal five years ago and asked him to update the market projections and best/worst-case scenarios for the industry.

Maria saw a familiar pattern emerge. The industry was projected to grow at a steady but unspectacular pace. The field was crowded with competitors creating 3D printing capabilities; a mix of major industrial firms and small start-ups, each fighting for a piece of the slowly growing pie while seeking a game-changing breakthrough. Customers broke into basically two segments – large manufactures who incorporated 3D printing technology into their exist-ing manufacturing lines, and suppliers to larger manufacturers who produced a dedicated component through this printing process. Neither appeared to be a good prospective client base. Maria could not understand why Percipience Ltd. would want in on this. Nevertheless, her team was adamant.

A week ago, the team had a much more heated discussion. Maria still thought the idea was clearly wrong while the team was unanimously in favor. They struggled to be cogent in their logic and Maria thought they had more passion than reason. She agreed to let them pitch the idea to the com-mittee; at a minimum Maria felt it would be a good learning experience.

Joe and Maria walked into the meeting room to find Maria's team and Chelsea already there. Two of the team were chatting over a laptop and two other team members were speaking in quiet, excited voices with Chelsea and furiously scrib-bling on a piece of paper. "Hi everyone, let's get started," Maria said.

After moving through an update on four other deals in various stages of realization, the meeting turned to the new 3D pitch. Billy Chan stood up to begin. Maria admired Billy and was glad he was on her team. She saw him as a broad thinker, very curious, and open. When this meeting was over, Maria was going to need to find a way to make him feel better.

Billy began to outline the business in which they wanted to acquire a part-nership stake – its financial condition, management, and product. When Billy said, "Now let me explain the opportunity," Joe interrupted.

"Billy, just so we're clear, for me to want Percipience Ltd. to enter the 3D printing control business, we would need to see a business case showing 7-10X returns in three years. I am having trouble seeing that from this com-pany." Maria nodded; she had already tried to explain this to the team.

Billy looked at Mike, his teammate driving the laptop, and at Chelsea; they exchanged a smile. Billy looked at Joe and Maria and said, "Clearly there is no way this target company can sell enough of this product, even with our help, to meet those returns. It's why we think creating a partnership to sell this product is a bad idea. But what about this?"

Mike tapped the keyboard and the logo for Alibaba, the largest retail marketplace in the world appeared on the screen, then Tencent, then Google Play. The screen continued to fill with logos. "We don't want to sell a product, we want to create a platform." Billy went on to paint a vision of a 3D printing platform that could support manufactures of all sizes and industries, providing the ability to blend standards, accessibility, and pricing advantages with the opportunity to integrate AI with human creativity.

Chelsea jumped in and excitedly began to describe the possibilities she saw. The meeting took an entirely different turn from what Maria had expected. She had anticipated a quick but polite rejection; however, the meeting turned into an animated brainstorming session and a set of action steps to move that idea forward.

After the meeting, Maria told her team that drinks after work were her treat and she followed Joe back to his office. "Well, I feel like an idiot," she said. "How did I miss that?"

"Join the club," sighed Joe. "At least you were open enough to let the team move forward with a pitch. I would have shut that down right out of the gate. At least we'll all look like geniuses when this turns into a billion-euro business," he joked.

After work, Maria stopped off at the pub to leave her credit card for the team as promised. Declining an offer to stay and celebrate, she hopped in her car and headed home. Sitting in traffic, she let out a sigh. "How did I nearly blow this?" she berated herself.

"How about if you stop beating yourself up and figure out how to learn from this mistake?" came the imagined voice of Frida Kahlo.

It was a significant mistake. I'm taking a moment to have some pity for myself, thought Maria. "Fine. Are you done?" retorted Kahlo. "Retrace your actions." Maria walked through what she had done after the first meeting – seeking out data, pulling together a picture of the landscape, and evaluating the opportunity. It all seemed right – but the outcome had been all wrong.

"It's not what you did but how you did it," reflected Frida. "Whose views did you seek out? What types of data did you use? What questions did you ask? What standards did you use? In each case, they were people whose views you already knew, extensions of data you already had, the same questions you have always asked. You managed to create your own little self-contained world. You're not working in an information bubble, it's an information castle – defending against anything original!"

Great. I can pop a bubble, thought Maria. How do I dismantle a castle? Frida chuckled sympathetically as her image faded away.

"I know what I know ... and I know I can prove it!" How many times have you thought like Maria: sure of what you know, assured that what has worked for you in the past will work in the future, confident that the voices of agreement that surround you are giving you good advice. But castles, unlike bubbles, don't just surround us, they protect us. When Maria was confronted with a novel, but uncertain idea, her information castle sprang to her defense – guarding her with information from the past and arming her with viewpoints that were already familiar. She used this perspective and experience to guard against an invasion of new information; comfortable in her arrogant confidence. Climbing beyond her castle walls required Maria to address reality: seeing what is actually there, putting it into an appropriate perspective, and bringing others together to collectively build an understanding of the present and the future.

THE VALUE OF ADDRESSING REALITY

As we have pointed out, the role of leadership is to "guide the tide," to have a positive impact on followers (Followership), the sustainable success of their organization (Sustainability), and the successful integration of technology and people in a way that maintains human dignity and creativity (Humanocity).

The chart below summarizes the outcomes that Addressing Reality creates in each of these areas as well as the skills discussed in this chapter that are needed to drive these outcomes (Figure 4.2).

Addressing Reality: Seeing the world as it is rather than as we wish it to be; the ability to separate fact from fiction and data from desire.		
FOLLOWERSHIP	**SUSTAINABILITY**	**HUMANOCITY**
Outcome: Creating common understanding	**Outcome:** Managing tension between long- and short-term objectives	**Outcome:** Creating meaningful ways to contribute
Skills: Managing biases to seek and interpret information	**Skills:** Systems thinking to bring the future into the present	**Skills:** Enrolling others to build common understanding

FIGURE 4.2
Addressing Reality

Information Castles

In order to make effective, consistent, and timely decisions, leaders tend to develop a "theory of the business." That is, a set of working assumptions about the factors that drive your part of the business to be successful and predictions about the likely impact to and response of our key stakeholders to the actions we take. These assumptions and predictions – your theory of the business – are built on the data you collect, the processes you use to analyze it, your own history and experiences, and the views of others you seek out. While intended to be a foundation for decisions, without constant attention, this mix of inputs can become insular and fixed – an information castle that shapes and limits your view of the world.

It is important to recognize that information castles are built on three types of reality: Objective reality, Subjective reality, and Intersubjective reality.

- Objective reality is true without the need for someone to perceive it: 2+2=4, bricks have mass, and X number of industrial manufacturers use 3D printing. However, as you may recognize, biases and our habits borne out of past experience and instinct can often lead us to distort objective reality.
- Subjective reality is based on your own set of beliefs and experiences: "$4 is a lot to pay for coffee"; "my yard would look better with a brick patio"; or "the growth curve for 3D printing is not attractive."
- Intersubjective reality consists of things that a group of people jointly believe to be true: "high quality sustainably farmed coffee is worth more than the alternative"; "good brick laying requires skilled professionals"; "creating a platform to support a fragmented industry is a viable business strategy that can be applied to 3D printing" (Figure 4.3).

All three realities are important – and are often mixed in the course of leadership experience. If you need to be reassured about the importance of subjective reality, just remember the last time someone asked you to judge an employee's performance and that judgment translated into a raise or bonus ... or a termination. If you need to be reassured about the

FIGURE 4.3
3 Types of Reality

importance of Intersubjective reality, just remember that you cannot eat, shelter under, or have sex with non-fungible tokens (NFTs), yet they have value simply because many people believe they have value. These three types of reality are the material we use to construct our information castles: the prism through which we interpret everything around us.

A leader's goal is to address reality by integrating these three perspectives; perceiving the world accurately enough to be able to see situations as they truly are, rather than how you wish them to be, separating fact from fiction and data from desire. It requires you to become sharply aware of your perceptual and cognitive systems and being aware of how you might be lured into making a mess of your perception. As Thomas Friedman wrote, "*The struggle between those seeking unexpected truths … and those worshiping alternative facts … is THE story…*"[1] (emphasis in the original).

The ability to address reality is a key skill that leaders need to guide the tide. Addressing reality allows you to:

- Translate purpose into strategy with a minimum of noise or distortion.
- Create a unifying vision and ways for followers to make meaningful contributions to the vision.
- Balance the tension between long- and short-term objectives.

While taking on this challenge requires you to deal simultaneously with objective, subjective, and intersubjective reality, let's begin by examining each of these realities separately.

Tackling Objective Reality – Seeing through the Fog of Your Own Wishes

"Two roads diverged in a wood and, and I – I took the one less traveled by, and that has made all the difference." Robert Frost's[2] advice on which road to take is well worth remembering. One of Maria Miller's missteps was forgetting this advice. As she sought out information to make a decision, she turned to familiar sources. It's a common choice, but a limiting one.

As Daniel Kahneman[3] reminded us, information about the "real world" comes to us with two features: noise and bias. Noise can be thought of as the stuff that undermines the credibility and reliability of the data – is it clean, does it contain irrelevant information, and is it accurate? One reason we turn to familiar sources of information is that we have already determined the source's reliability and credibility and so we know how to judge the value of the information we receive. According to Kahneman, noise distorts objective reality in unpredictable, non-systematic ways.

The other reason we turn to familiar sources is that we are comfortable – perhaps too comfortable – with the perspective and underlying bias that the source will use to shape the information we receive. This is how bias creates systemic distortions. For example, a sales team may seek to collect data from customers to project sales. They may do this through conversations, pre-orders, and past purchasing patterns – all these avenues will contain some "noise" – incorrect estimates from customers, misinterpreted conversations, etc. The data will contain some lack of reliability. Knowing this, the sales team, which may be more concerned with out-of-stock issues than excess inventory and be confident in their ability to drive sales, may report their projections using the highest estimates from the collected data – this is bias.

Despite what received wisdom would tell us about the power of rational thinking, neurological research tells us that we respond to messages that we receive not only with our critical reasoning skills but also with our emotions. Familiar, expected information and new information that conforms to our world view – what psychologists call our "assumptive schema"[4] – generate positive, reinforcing emotions while information that does not fit with our assumptive schema generate unpleasant emotions. Not surprisingly, unless we are actively working to seek out information from novel sources, we tend to fall back on those sources that are familiar and reinforcing.

The need to be right is part of an ancient survival mechanism that favors biases which save energy. Making the cognitive effort required to challenge these biases costs energy. As we mentioned earlier, nature loves shortcuts and it is no surprise that cognitive shortcuts are a big part of our shared evolutionary history. The human brain – although a mere three pounds in weight – consumes an inordinate amount of the body's energy: more than 20%. One-third of that energy is used for simple "maintenance" and two-thirds for thinking, fueling electrical impulses that neurons employ to communicate with each other.[5] The bottom line is that evolution has introduced a default system to conserve energy, which includes our biases, habits, and even our instincts. While this system allows you to be efficient – biases *do* save time – it makes it more difficult to see objective reality. We require considerable cognitive effort to overcome this default.

To address these problems, it is necessary to actively, continually seek out new and novel sources. Doing so means accepting the need to "qualify" the data sources, that is to try to understand the noise inherent in the source. More challenging: it means accepting the discomfort of information that is presented from a different perspective, with different biases than your own. It means enlarging your assumptive schema.

Coming to Terms with Subjective Reality – Moving from Data to Insight

"What is going on?" is the question objective reality seeks to answer. "What does this mean?" is the question subjective reality seeks to answer. Subjective reality is where our experiences and judgment translate data (Objective reality) into insight. Creating insight requires you to interpret information by assessing the data you've acquired with judgment grounded in critical reason rather than in emotion or prior beliefs. Addressing this challenge productively allows you to assess complex sets of facts and data and then communicate them in a clear and meaningful way.

Subjective reality is dangerous because it requires you to make a choice; it prompts you to choose the high road *or* the low road. The low road of subjective reality is one in which the judgment you use in translating data to insight is driven by anxieties and personal ambitions, while the high road is one in which your judgment is driven by your values. In the situation with Maria described above, her concerns about repeating a past failure lead her to translate the idea her team brought her as a trap to be avoided. Her colleague, Chelsea, based her judgment instead on the purpose of the committee: a value of seeking out innovation, and translated the same data into a transformative opportunity.

Let's look first at the low road. We will begin with an example which may feel familiar, an example we have seen often, retold as an incident in Maria's career.

A MARIA MOMENT

"Damn it!" Maria strode into her office, closed the door, and flung the binder she was holding onto her desk, sending a coffee mug flying to the floor, where it shattered. "Damn it!"

Pat, her colleague and next-door office neighbor tapped on Maria's door and walked in, Everything OK?" she asked. Maria looked up from picking up the shards of coffee mug at "imperturbable Pat" as Maria thought of her. A hurricane could rip the roof off the building and Pat would just shrug. That was not always a good thing but today, perhaps, it was just what Maria needed.

"He did it again, and she did it again!" Maria muttered through gritted teeth. "Once more, so I can understand," said Pat.

"I just came out of the planning meeting and in the middle of laying out the three targets for next quarter, Mike pipes up and says he was meeting with Nancy yesterday and she is not going to support our second target. I am sick and tired of our boss meeting with my staff behind my back," steamed Maria.

"Yes, Nancy does this with everyone," Pat responded flatly.

"I know. And most of my team has the good sense to give me a heads up, but Mike just loves the attention and delights in pulling the 'Nancy card'."

Pat paused to let some of Maria's anger defuse and then said, "Fuming about it is not going to help. Instead, maybe think of this as data. Everyone's actions and emotions too, are data. Try to think about why they are acting and feeling this way. What is Mike getting out of doing this? Why does Nancy act this way? Once you get a handle on that, you can take it into account and use what you've learned as data to help move your objectives forward."

"That's an interesting way to think about this, and I will," Maria said as she tossed the broken pieces of mug into the trash. "As soon as I stop being angry!"

The low road can be triggered by a variety of factors including stress, anxiety, arrogance, hubris, and even experience. More than 70 years ago, Karen Horney[6] described three non-productive ways in which people relate to others when driven by anxiety, concern, and stress: *Moving Away* from others, which involves creating social and emotional distance, that is, withdrawing; *Moving Against* others, which involves either overwhelming or dominating others, that is, aggression; and *Moving Toward* others, which involves becoming overly close and dependent upon others, that is, ingratiation. These three approaches remain one of the most popular frameworks to assess and coach leaders in danger of derailment.[7]

When we use one of these strategies as a lens through which to create our subjective reality, we are left with a limited, and indeed sometimes harmful approach to the world. For example, *"Tom is out of the office today (fact). I am not sure he cares about the new sales figures and can wait until the meeting tomorrow"* (Moving Away); or *"Tom made a mistake in that LinkedIn post (fact), tracking how many people notice will be a good way to find out if anyone pays attention to what he writes"* (Moving Against), or *"The new sales figures are out (fact), I'd better go meet with Tom to find out what he wants me to say about them"* (Moving Toward).

The high road of subjective reality is one where you make the choice to engage with productive needs. Productive needs facilitate the sense-making process that is so vital, especially when dealing with high levels of ambiguity. They are an invaluable compass we all carry inside us. Just as the low road is shaped by your motivation to avoid fears and anxiety, the high road is shaped by the ways you are motivated to be productive.[8]

One widely researched and respected framework for understanding productive needs suggests that, within a leadership context, the needs for affiliation (building good, secure relationships), achievement, and power (working through and directing others) are the primary drivers that motivate us.[9] More recent research has suggested relatedness (very similar to affiliation), competence, and autonomy (self-direction of activity) as key drivers.[10] Taken together, understanding these five needs – affiliation/relatedness, achievement, power, autonomy, and competence – can shape productive values.

Just as in your efforts to effectively "see" objective reality, subjective reality – effectively turning objective reality into meaning – requires that you be aware of what is driving your judgment about the data. Are they productive needs or are they being driven by fears and anxieties. The high road is easily missed as you try and navigate through life rushed and harried, dealing with so many things at any given time. Rather, the high road emerges into view when you can reach out and connect with what really matters to you. If the low road pushes your need to be right, the high road implores and guides you to do the right thing.

Effectively making sense out of the world around you – creating a productive Subjective reality – positions us to deal with Intersubjective reality.

Intersubjective Reality: Enrolling Others

Intersubjective reality, that set of beliefs that a group of people jointly hold, represents a great opportunity for leaders. It provides the space for you to truly bring others together by fostering conversations on the way they see the world today and the way it can be tomorrow. Bringing others into a purpose-driven vision and truly enrolling them in a productive joint effort requires what Robert Kegan[11] called "systems thinking." Systems thinking is a sophisticated approach to looking at reality. Let's work our way up to this and start with an unsophisticated approach. *"My views are important"* (egocentric thinking) is a typical perspective of the petulant child (or executive or politician), driven only to achieve their own aims and satisfy their own egos.

"My views are important, and they impact others" (subjective thinking) is a bit more sophisticated. It implies the ability to see the consequences of your conversations, actions, and behaviors. This is a level of thinking that helps you see cause and effect and is often used to drive a project or agenda. However, it falls woefully short when it comes to guiding the tide, as it comes from a preoccupation with the barriers and obstacles that prevent you from achieving your agenda. This type of thinking, all too common, forces you into the inertia of a limited perspective where everyone else needs to either *"get on the bus or get out of the way."*

"My views are important as they impact others and alter their views," AND *"their views in turn impact me and alter my views,"* AND *"through our conversations and dialogue, we elevate our thinking and we begin to work together to form a shared perspective of common purpose"* is a far more sophisticated way of approaching reality. This is the heart of systems thinking conversations: the recognition of, and the ability to create, a shared reality. It is vital for guiding the tide for three reasons.

First, your relationships move from being extrinsically valuable to intrinsically valuable.[12] When you see your views as both primary and impacting others, you may see others as tools to be used to further your views, which is what Kegan terms extrinsically valuable. But once you grab hold of the idea of actively creating a joint (Intersubjective) reality – others become intrinsically valuable – their worth, their value, and their perspective become equal to your own; there is no longer a hierarchy of value. This deep appreciation for the value of others will enable you to fully utilize the creative, aesthetic, and cultural perspectives of those around you. Keep in mind that this cannot and will not be possible unless you create an environment where everyone feels safe to speak openly and freely, expressing their views in the spirit of contribution rather than challenge. As authors such as Amy Edmondson[13] and the late (great) Ed Schein[14] have pointed out, true contribution is not possible without a culture of psychological safety.

Second, systems thinking helps you gain the ability to connect with others' needs and motivations more fully. Rather than "dealing" with others' needs, a systems perspective allows you to create a common way of understanding the world that guides action and judgment. This becomes possible once you begin to build shared meaning through a mutual relationship rather than separate points of view that simply co-exist.

Finally, systems thinking causes the way you plan and see the future to change dramatically. When you see the world only from a subjective thinking perspective, the future becomes a version of the present that has not yet occurred: an extension of what you are doing now. But, when you take a systems perspective and operate in an Intersubjective reality, you can see novel, more creative versions of the future. Perhaps even more importantly, you can see the future as present right now. The path to building an innovative future from your existing present becomes apparent, leading to a greater ability to balance long- and short-term demands, seeing new possibilities, and creating a hope-centered vision for action.

It may seem a bit odd in a discussion about Addressing Reality to be talking about bringing the future into the present. Especially when the goal of Addressing Reality is to see the world the way it is, not how we wish it to be. However, taking the future into account is necessary, even critical if you are to truly be able to Address Reality. The great danger in failing to Address Reality is to become enmeshed – even emboldened – by a deluded sense of certitude. Recognizing that we can guide but not control the tide of forces within which we operate is one way to avoid this unwarranted sense of certitude. A second is to do the work to see the world the way it actually is by integrating objective, subjective, and intersubjective realities.

The third task in Addressing Reality, the one that requires us to take the future into account, is mindfulness.

Approaching the World by Being Mindful

The term "mindfulness" can often lead us to focus on the idea of being present. Certainly, we see this as important, though we believe it as only one aspect of mindfulness. For our purposes, we define mindfulness as having four facets:[15]

- *Situational Awareness* – seeing the whole picture, all of the factors that are impacting the moment, without blinders.
- *Self-Awareness* – recognizing your own actions and assumptions, and the impact they have on others.
- *Temporal Awareness* – being present, acting on, and being in the moment.
- *Peripheral Awareness*– recognizing and attending to trends that are developing "over the horizon."

Situational Awareness is an aspect of mindfulness that allows you to deal with objective reality. We are talking about being fully conscious of everything that can have direct influence on the matter at hand, that is, seeing the whole field and taking action on what is happening rather than reacting to what you think has happened. Building situational awareness requires that you remove the blinders that limit the sources of information you seek out and expand your view of what is relevant.

Self-Awareness allows you to productively engage with Subjective Reality. As we discussed above, needs and values create the lens through which you interpret objective reality. The goal is to be aware of and focus on productive needs and values. How do you remain self-aware? One solution is to recognize that acting in ways consistent with your values makes you feel comfortable, while acting in ways that are inconsistent will make you uncomfortable. You can take advantage of this by periodically asking yourself two questions: "How do I feel about what I am doing?" and "Why?" If you are comfortable with the way you are addressing a challenge, you should be asking yourself: "*Is this the most effective way to proceed or simply the one I always use? What might someone choose to do differently and how might that work out?*" If you are feeling uncomfortable with your actions, ask yourself: "*Am I acting productively but in a way that is new and* *stretching me, or am I acting in ways that are inconsistent with who I am because I am being pressured to do so?"*

Temporal Awareness allows you to engage productively with Inter-subjective reality. Temporal awareness is about being present, acting on, and being in the moment. The lack of temporal awareness – mindlessness – is a common, pervasive, and potentially destructive way of being. When you act mindlessly, a common event can trigger an automatic reaction and you may not even be fully aware that you are reacting. It's a bit like driving down a familiar route and realizing you don't remember the drive, eating a meal and not remembering putting the fork in your mouth, or having a familiar conversation with your spouse and snapping to in the middle of it asking, *"What were we talking about?"* Remaining present is what allows you not to fall back on familiar, automatic ways of thinking and to actively engage with others: understanding where they are coming from rather than reacting to them in pre-programmed, thoughtless ways.

Finally, **Peripheral Awareness** is the aspect of mindfulness that calls you to look over the horizon and bring the future into the present. The need to peek over the horizon, to recognize weak signals as Nate Silver calls them,[16] is critical to balancing long- and short-term demands. How do you do this? Cultivating a habit of curiosity is one of the best approaches to building peripheral awareness. Think about the course of your typical workweek. How many people do you speak with who are not in your industry and profession? What circle are you drawing your inputs and stimuli from? How many things do you read that are not directly relevant to your immediate activities? Increasing this number is a first step in cultivating a habit of curiosity, which will increase your Peripheral Awareness.

IN SUMMARY

Across this chapter, we have been taking on the challenge of seeing the world as it is … and as we want it to become, rather than simply seeing what we want to see. It's a complex process of: (1) actively seeking information in the realm of objective reality, (2) turning data into meaning by interpreting information in the world of subjective reality, and (3) bringing others into a common understanding by enrolling them in the collaborative work of inter subjective reality. Throughout this effort, maintaining mindfulness – of ourselves, the full present, and what is lurking over the horizon – fuels our ability to develop a story of the future that is creative, compelling, and feels present right now.

Below is a summary of the key concepts we have introduced in describing the practice of Addressing Reality (Figure 4.4).

The next morning, Billy dropped by Maria's office to return her credit card. "Thanks for the drinks," he said.

"My pleasure," Maria smiled back. "I spent the night thinking about that meeting. I guess I was thinking about this opportunity the wrong way. Thanks for showing me the light."

"Not the wrong way, but maybe a familiar way," Billy said. "Isn't that why you keep us around, to shake things up?"

"The next time you see me fall into old patterns, throw a book at me or something, will ya?" Maria smiled.

"No problem, boss!" laughed Billy as he walked away.　　　　　•

ADDRESSING REALITY	
Seeing the world as it is rather than as we wish it to be; the ability to separate fact from fiction and data from desire.	
CONCEPT SUMMARY	
Seeking Information	An active effort directed towards seeking out multiple credible sources rather than passively accepting ideas, the key task in dealing with objective reality.
Interpreting Information	Assessing the data we've acquired with judgment grounded in critical reason rather than in emotion or prior beliefs, the key task in dealing with subjective reality.
Enrolling Others	Bringing others into a purpose-driven vision, bringing people together in the way they see the world today and the way it can be tomorrow, the key goal of intersubjective reality.
Maintaining Mindfulness	Actively choosing to live in the present (Temporal Awareness), to see the whole field (Situational Awareness), to peer over the horizon (Peripheral Awareness), and to recognize our own impact on the situation (Self Awareness) – all at once.
Deluded Certitude	The unshakable belief in one's convictions, without testing them against reality, brought about by hubris and misdirected passion.

FIGURE 4.4
Addressing Reality Concept Summary

It's good that the team has my back, but I think I may need to make breaking my thinking patterns a priority for myself, *thought Maria as she turned her attention to the next matter.* Besides, Billy's aim is too good.

NOTES

1 Thomas L. Friedman, "How to Stop Trump and Prevent Another Jan. 6," *The New York Times* (Jan. 5, 2022), New York edition, sec. A.

2 Robert Frost, "The Road Not Taken and Other Poems," *The Atlantic Monthly* (Aug. 1915), https://www.theatlantic.com/magazine/archive/1915/08/a-group-of-poems/306620/.

3 Daniel Kahneman A.M. Rosenfield, L. Gandhi, and T. Blaser, "Noise: How to Overcome the High, Hidden Cost of Inconsistent Decision Making" *Harvard Business Review* (Oct. 2016).

4 Ronnie Janoff-Bulman, "Assumptive Worlds and the Stress of Traumatic Events: Applications of the Schema Construct," *Social Cognition* 7, no. 2 (Jun. 1989): 113–36, https://doi.org/10.1521/soco.1989.7.2.113.

5 Nikhil Swaminathan, "Why Does the Brain Need So Much Power?" *Scientific American* (Apr. 29, 2008), https://www.scientificamerican.com/article/why-does-the-brain-need-s/.

6 Karen Horney, *The Collected Works of Karen Horney*, vol. 1, 2 vols (New York: W. W. Norton Inc., 1937).

7 Robert Hogan R.B. Kaiser, R.A. Sherman, and P.D. Harms, "Twenty Years on the Dark Side: Six Lessons about Bad Leadership.," *Consulting Psychology Journal: Practice and Research* 73, no. 3 (Sept. 2021): 199–213, https://doi.org/10.1037/cpb0000205.

8 Frank Guglielmo and Sudhanshu Palsule, *The Social Leader: Redefining Leadership for the Complex Social Age* (Brookline, MA: Bibliomotion, 2014).

9 David C. McClelland, *Human Motivation*, Re-issued digitally printed version (Cambridge: Cambridge University Press, 2009).

10 Edward L. Deci and Richard M. Ryan, "The 'What' and 'Why' of Goal Pursuits: Human Needs and the Self-Determination of Behavior," *Psychological Inquiry* 11, no. 4 (Nov. 2009): 227–68, https://doi.org/10.1207/S15327965PLI1104_01.

11 Robert Kegan, *In over Our Heads: The Mental Demands of Modern Life* (Cambridge, MA: Harvard University Press 1994).

12 Robert Kegan, *In over Our Heads: The Mental Demands of Modern Life* (Cambridge, MA: Harvard University Press 1994).

13 Amy Edmondson, *The Fearless Organization: Creating Psychological Safety in the Workplace for Learning Innovation and Growth* (Hoboken, NJ: John Wiley & Sons, 2018).

14 Schein, Edgar H. & Bennis W.G. Organizational Change Through Group Methods: The Laboratory Approach. Wiley 1965.

15 Guglielmo and Palsule, *The Social Leader.*

16 Nate Silver, *The Signal and the Noise: Why So Many Predictions Fail – but Some Don't*, Published with a new preface in Penguin Books Economics/Politics/Sports (New York Penguin Books, 2020).

5

Adaptive Impact

The challenge of creating successful execution, leading the team and one's self forward in a way that creates success and ongoing relevance (Figure 5.1).

HONEST ENGAGEMENT	**ADDRESSING REALITY**	**ADAPTIVE IMPACT**
Purpose	Seeking & Interpreting Information	Stepping into the Tide
Values		Ambitious Realism
Empathy	Enrolling Others	Managing the Talent Challenge
	Maintaining Mindfulness	

FIGURE 5.1
Guiding the Tide Practices: Adaptive Impact

DOI: 10.4324/9781003491880-5

WHERE MARIA LEARNS WHERE THE LEVERAGE POINT IS

"I'm sorry, Laurent is in a meeting and his calendar is full this week, do you want me to look for some time next week?"

"No," said Maria. "Just tell him I called and ask him to ring me if he has a minute."

Great, *thought Maria*. What good is it for your new boss to tell you he has an open door if there is always a long line in front of it?

Maria was a week into her first senior appointment at Percipience Ltd. She'd been promoted to Head of Customer Experience. Getting the appointment felt like she had finally "made it." But the honeymoon had faded fast. Her team, spread across the EU, seemed frustrated and disengaged. Laurent, her new boss, was enthusiastic but never available.

Maria turned her attention back to getting an accurate picture of the department she'd inherited. It was clear that the group had been underperforming for some time. Just today, Maria had gained access to her predecessor's emails and the number of complaints and concerns was surprising. Then she came upon a set of emails that drained the color from her face. The "official" story was that her predecessor had left for a new opportunity, but the reality the emails told was different: she had been fired for missing her targets.

It soon became clear to Maria that the situation was far worse than she had thought. "There is a culture of under-performance here, and it is because no one ever gives tough feedback to anyone." Those were the parting words of a team member who had given in his papers before Maria had joined and had just finished out his notice period.

Frida, what did I get myself into? *thought Maria.*

As often happened, the image of Frida Kahlo popped into Maria's head for a conversation.

"Come on now," said Frida, "you knew what you were stepping into. Everyone knew this group was in trouble. How did you feel when they offered you the job?"

"Proud, optimistic, and confident I could make a difference," Maria responded. "But at the same time, humbled by the opportunity. And I'm worried that humility is now turning into desperation."

Just then Maria's phone rang, and she had to turn her attention away from Frida.

After resolving the fire drill of the moment, Maria picked up a pencil and decided to stop wallowing. She sketched out a simple SWOT analysis of her

---

Customer Experience: Rough SWOT

STRENGTHS
- Proven team, few weak players
- Strong reputation - client service
- Boss, Laurent - big supporter
- Marketing Lead, Pedro - extreme talent
- Personal experience/track record
- European economic climate
- Approved Headcount: Strategy + Analytics Lead

WEAKNESSES
- Oscar (prev. incumbent) was terminated
- Team is dispirited from poor leadership and performance
- Boss, Laurent - actually focused on own survival
- Weak HR support over time: "tough client"
- Lack of performance over time has stressed team, teamwork
- All existing headcount frozen
- Strategy + Analytics Lead opening on a clock: "use it or lose it"

OPPORTUNITIES
- Team members - strong talent and ambition
- Catalyze this group as a "team" = major power
- Turnaround will be noticed, major contributor to NOW
- Stated support of Laurent (not yet called on)
- Springboard for own career - success could lead to...
- Strategy + Analytics Lead could pole vault the team

THREATS
- Strong market for CS folks; external opportunities for the team
- If Pedro leaves, may start an exodus
- Previous incumbent terminated - "no pressure!"
- Six quarters of losses - not much runway left, tick tock
- Will Laurent support me in the long term?
- If new Strategy + Analytics hire fails, will be highly visible setback

---

FIGURE 5.2
Customer Experience Rough SWOT

division and saw that she needed to go after hiring a Head of Strategy and Analysis (Figure 5.2).

"This is my opportunity," Maria said out loud. She thought, I can use this hire to change the story of the group – how we think about our impact on the business, reset our shared ambitions, and, at the same time, elevate some diverse voices.

The next day, Maria set out to personally lead the search. She started by asking her team for input on the job profile; she wanted to make everyone feel included. She also used these conversations to communicate her values and the skills she expected from her team across her department: focus, results, and accountability. Maria wanted to shake up the division *and bring in someone who could drive results. She found her ideal candidate in John who had headed up strategy at a competitor's firm. When she read the comment by the HR lead in the interviews that John "may be a little rough around the edges," she smiled to herself and thought that this was precisely the kind of person she needed to show her team what tough looked like.*

As time went by, Maria began depending more and more on John. Their meetings often ran late into the evening, as they discussed everything from the numbers to the other members of the team. John had introduced some new clever processes that were tracking performance on a weekly basis. He had also brought in a consulting firm to implement a change management program and Maria was impressed by their ideas. Over the next six months, her division had an entirely new structure with new roles and reporting lines. The results were better too, and some of the savings came from redundancies that had been swiftly eliminated.

A year had passed since Maria had stepped into her role, six months since the changes she, John, and his consultants had planned were implemented. Maria found herself sitting at her desk about to open an email from HR with the results of her team's annual Engagement survey. As she waited for the survey results to download, she reflected that, over the last year, some aspects of the troubled department she'd inherited were better. The team was leaner and results were certainly improved. But some things were worse than before, for instance, the way people seemed to feel about their work and their relationships at work.

When the file finally opened, it dawned on Maria how poorly things were going. The scores had tanked badly, and the worst cut of all for Maria was reading the answers to the question, "Would the team members recommend Percipience as a place to work to their friends?" The answer was a resounding NO from almost every member of her team.

Later that same day, Laurent walked into her office. Maria was sitting at her desk gazing out of the window. She had worked very, very hard for the past year to produce the results she was brought in to deliver, and she had done that. But clearly her effort was not enough. Maria's face wore that look of concern and disappointment that Laurent had come to know well whenever Maria felt that she was failing.

"What's the matter?" Laurent asked in a casual tone. Maria shared with him the findings of the Engagement Survey. Laurent smiled at her and said, "Results mean much more than just the numbers, Maria. The numbers are important and without them, we don't exist. But there is much more than

the numbers when it comes to results. How you deliver them is just as important as whether you hit your targets. You need to focus on people and the talent that we want in our business and the resources you spend to hit your results too." He added, "You have done a good job, but you can do a lot better." Laurent smiled and offered to help any time she wanted as he headed out the door.

"Well, what the hell do you make of that, Frida?" sighed Maria.

"I think he was saying you need to think about today and tomorrow," replied the image of Frida Kahlo as she reclined against the window.

"What does that mean?" shot back Maria.

"What do you think?" responded Frida.

Maria found herself pondering Frida's question, and then she remembered a scene from a movie that had deeply impacted her years ago. It took Maria a while to remember the movie title, The Legend of Bagger Vance, *a story set in the Great Depression of the 1930s about a gifted golfer who had lost his swing. A war veteran, he allows the stresses of his life to take over his ability for perspective. Struggling and failing during a tournament, he is confronted by his caddy – much like Maria's Frida – who stops him and asks him a question, "Do you see the field?" That question had remained etched in Maria's mind.*

The field the wise caddy was describing was not just the 18-hole course, but the larger field in which we are called upon to play our role to the best of our abilities. "A man's grip on his club is just like his grip on the world ... it's somewhere in the harmony of all that is, all that was, all that will be,"[1] exhorts the caddy.

Maria swiveled away from the window toward her desk, picked up a pen, and scribbled, "What am I not seeing?"

"Welcome to the real conversation," said Frida as she faded from Maria's thoughts.

No matter what our role, the pressure to deliver results is always with us, demanding our attention and focus. That's as it should be; delivering today's results matters a great deal. But as Maria experienced, delivering for today cannot take all of your attention, perhaps not even the majority of it. With her team in crisis, Maria took several steps to address the problem – she stepped forward and took action, she recognized that the quality of talent on the team would set the pace of her success, and she imbued the team with ambition. Yet with her focus on delivering results for today, she created potentially debilitating challenges for the future. Her focus was on delivering, even exceeding, the expected results; not on achieving results-beyond-results.

WHAT IS ADAPTIVE IMPACT?

Adaptive Impact is about delivering results-beyond-results. By results-beyond-results, we mean delivering the immediate targeted results such as KPIs, OKRs, AOI, and NPS, while simultaneously delivering results in the following three additional areas:

- Followership – Coalescing human energy by creating a direction and a momentum that others will seek to follow.
- Sustainability – Delivering value in a way that outpaces the resources consumed and continually exploring innovative ways of crafting the future.
- Humanocity – Combining the potential of human creativity with the efficiency and speed of automation, creating more than any one person could individually.

The practice of Adaptive Impact centers around the idea of seeing yourself as the author of the story that is unfolding around you, rather than as a character merely driven along by the plot. However – and this is a big however – the practice of Adaptive Impact requires you to approach the idea of writing your story with humility. This is the humility to recognize that your story exists within the tide which is something that cannot be controlled, but can be shaped.

In order to guide the tide through Adaptive Impact, you must do three things. First, you must step into the tide, finding the critical pivot point where it is possible to cause a meaningful disruption. Once you step into the tide, you must embody what we call Ambitious Realism, that is, a new story, a compelling narrative of the future while making sure that others feel included in the journey. Finally, you must meet the talent challenge of ensuring that both yourself and the others around you remain continually relevant to meeting the opportunities on the horizon.

Acting within the Tide

"The harmony of all that is, all that was, and all that will be..."[2]

Inevitably, we have no choice in life but to deal with three stories at once: the story that was, the story that is, and the story that will be, or rather *can* be. But it is so easy to lose perspective in pursuit of the immediate problem to fix – the story of *what is*. The human brain – once it goes on high alert – is programmed to lose the broad perspective and focus entirely on the danger at hand. While this evolutionary inheritance is an excellent technique for survival during immediate danger, if it is not managed, it prevents our ability to bring perspective. In the story above, Maria did act, but her action was blind to what had led Percipience Ltd. and her department to where it was (the story of *what was*). She was also blind to what was emerging out there in the world of technology that would have an impact on what was emerging in the *"what will be/can be"*. In other words, she ignored the tide.

Guiding the Tide is about the ability to deal with the demands of the here and now, while, at the same time, working to build what can be. Your organization is at the confluence of the three stories described above. As a leader, your perspective must include all three narratives. KPIs, OKRs, AOI, NPS, and the rest are in the field of immediate vision, but the field has to be greater and wider than these measures. Success in the immediate does offer us a quick tangible reward, but it hardly guarantees relevance in an emergent and fast-changing world. Without building followership, sustainable execution, and Humanocity, immediate results are bound to be fleeting.

Take a look at some of the demands of 21st-century organizations on leaders and decide for yourself if it is possible to be successful focusing only on the immediate without accounting for the tide.

Shrinking zones of influence

Leaders will have increasingly narrower zones of direct influence owing to flatter organizations, smaller organizational units, and higher local empowerment with deep and expansive interconnections both within and across the organization. Therefore, a leader's role will increasingly be about creating meaning rather than setting direction. Organizations are frequently reflecting this through what is thought of as "freedom within a framework". Driving change, accomplishing a goal, or achieving a desired end state requires leaders to find ways to establish the widest possible range of freedom to act by respecting and leveraging the complex interdependencies of the matrix. Rather than the reactive stance of *organizational agility*, leaders will need to leverage and shape the complexity rather than simply react to it.

Local versus system optimization balancing act

Trends toward systems optimization rather than "unit" optimization – that is, avoiding sub-optimization – will become more nuanced. Traditionally, systems at all levels – from globalized supply chains to organizational-level decisions – have favored the overall optimal performance of the system over the optimal performance of the sub-units. For example, supply chains are sourced globally and work is moved to lower labor cost markets to create the least possible cost of goods sold (COGS) for a finished product (system optimization). This occurs at the expense of local workers or local producers who are often shrunk or driven out of business (local optimization). This will inevitably become a much subtler balancing decision as accounting for externalities (the costs an organization imposes on its environment) becomes a more routine part of business decisions.

Zoom lens perspective

As leaders become unable to focus solely on system optimization, they will need to take a more nuanced and flexible perspective of situations to make more thoughtfully responsive decisions. This requires leaders to be skilled at both zooming into local details and zooming out to see the big picture.

The "freight train"

We are seeing an increase in socially created information propelled by the global interconnectivity of cheap mass communication media. This, in turn, is fueled by ever more sophisticated actors that will create what we call a "freight train" where trends, ideas, and movements gather speed and momentum faster than ever before.

Defining the digital line

The rise of AI and its continued evolution will call on leaders to continually consider the answers to the how, where (and why) work is accomplished. The build/buy/borrow/bot leadership decision will be more than a clinical business call based on what is most efficient and cost-effective for the short and mid-term. Increasing opportunities for automation and replacement of humans will call on considerations of both ethics (in which decisions should humans be involved?) and values (how are leaders considering workers, their lives, and careers and maintaining the diversity of thought to drive innovation?).

Adaptive Impact is the relentless endeavor to keep in mind the three stories we described above (what was, what is, and what could be) in order to build the resources to stay relevant in a rapidly changing world, deliver value in a way that outpaces the resources we are consuming, and create the conditions that bring out the best in the people we lead.

In the prior chapters, our focus has been on the "inside-out" practices of Guiding the Tide. Honest Engagement was all about this inside-out perspective. Addressing Reality similarly has an inside-out trajectory, beginning with yourself and then reaching out to engage with the wider world, proactively moving through complexity and ambiguity. Now with Adaptive Impact, the focus shifts entirely to the outside-in perspective: this requires you to both **begin and end outside of yourself.**

The alternative to Adaptive Impact is to become "stuck in neutral." Leaders who are stuck in neutral lead their teams and organizations to continually deliver the same outcomes, making modest, continual, incremental improvements along the way. Such an approach eventually costs the organization more (either directly or through opportunity costs) over time than it delivers. Stuck in neutral is a state in which not only do you fail to address fundamental challenges but you also lose the perspective of the tide, forgetting what was and what could be. Being stuck in neutral means adapting yourself to a position in which you ignore the tide and focus on the immediate challenges and, for the sake of comfort and continuity, become "comfortably numb" in the process.

The Components of Adaptive Impact

Adaptive Impact is the practice of stepping into the tide in order to drive the organization, team, and yourself forward in a way that creates sustainable success and ongoing relevance (Figure 5.3). You can build this practice through:

- **Stepping into the tide** – locating the critical pivot point where the complex components of the tide meet and creating a meaningful disruption to shape the flow. This is accomplished through:
  - The Humble Safari, reaching out and learning about the organization beyond your formal accountabilities.
  - Challenging the group schema, asking the difficult questions to surface underlying assumptions, and testing the "why."

Adaptive Impact: Leading the organization, team, and one's self forward in a way that creates sustainable success and on-going relevance.		
FOLLOWERSHIP	**SUSTAINABILITY**	**HUMANOCITY**
Outcome: Coalescing human energy and momentum	**Outcome:** Creating more value than is consumed	**Outcome:** Integrating human aesthetic with the efficiency of technology
Skills: Stepping into the tide via the Humble Safari and challenging the group schema	**Skills:** Embodying ambitious realism through personal visibility and creating inclusion	**Skills:** Meeting the talent challenge through Dynamic Curiosity and Curating Capabilities

FIGURE 5.3
Adaptive Impact

- **Embodying Ambitious Realism** – helping others come together in defining an ambitious future that is both grounded in reality and considered worth striving for by everyone you lead. This is accomplished through:
  - Inclusion.
  - Being visible, creating, and telling the story – building a compelling narrative of the future.
- **Meeting the Talent Challenge** – ensuring that you and those others around you remain continually relevant to meet the opportunities on the horizon. This is accomplished through:
  - Dynamic Curiosity – remaining in a constant state of incompletion, shifting your perspective from: Know it all to Learn it all
  - Curating Capabilities – continually scanning and comparing the demands of the environment to your own strengths and to continually refine the list of requisite skills – then doing the work to develop those skills.

Stepping into the Tide

The tide is the metaphor we are using to describe an environment in continuous flow and largely impervious to our command and control. The tide occupies a wide space and there are rarely clear markers on where we can have an impact, disrupting the flow of the tide, thereby guiding its course. The challenge is to find that place. We are mixing metaphors here, but we are reminded of that famous quote from Archimedes: "*Give me a lever and a place to stand, and I will move the earth.*" The trick is to find that place to stand; it means finding that place in the moving tide where your actions are likely to have the maximum impact. We call the search for that place the Humble Safari.

The Humble Safari

How do we go about finding that place to stand and create leverage? Leaders usually have good visibility into their own areas of accountability and the areas adjacent to them. As we noted, the tide is wide. Journeying beyond your own accountabilities is the only way to come to locate the leverage points in the tide. This expedition, this "safari" across the organization, requires that you go forth with a humble mindset. This is an adventure in which you seek to learn, to see problems from new perspectives while uncovering new challenges and opportunities.

The danger is to approach the safari with the intention of bringing new data into your existing way of seeing the world, or worse, thinking only in terms of how anything new you learn impacts your immediate challenges. Your goal must be to broaden your understanding. Humility and curiosity are the hallmarks of a successful safari across the organization. Let's look at a famous example of a successful humble safari.

Satya Nadella's most important step once he took over as the CEO of Microsoft was to simply listen. "*I heard from hundreds of employees at every level and in every part of the company. We held focus groups to allow people to share their opinions anonymously as well. Listening was the most important thing I accomplished each day, because it would build the foundation of my leadership for years to come.*"[3] Nadella was exploring the three questions: what was, what is, and what can be. As a Microsoft lifer, Nadella could have easily assumed that he knew the company like the back of his hand. He did not. Instead, he created his own Humble Safari and stepped into the tide!

Stepping into the tide is first and foremost about accepting a state of not-knowing where exactly the optimal point of impact may be located. The temptation, of course, is to act – to take decisions, get going, announce a strategy, get the team organized, assign KPIs – the list is virtually endless. But the Humble Safari is quite different. The ability to say, "I don't know," is the most important aspect of the Humble Safari. Yes, you may have an informed point of view and we are not suggesting that you start off with a completely clean slate. Test your point of view, hang out with those who disagree with you, and find out why. Then – challenge the group schema!

Challenging the Group Schema

The reason you need to step into the tide is to create the purposeful disruption that shifts the direction of that tide. If the goal of the humble safari is to find the point in the tide where maximum leverage can be created, the point of challenging the assumptive schema is to begin the disruption by changing the way others think about the tide. The history of a group, department, or organization – the story of what was – brings with it a set of assumptions about how the tide works and why. When stepping into the tide, a leader challenges these fundamental assumptions – the "assumptive schema" – of the group. The humble safari will surface the key assumptions. Now it is time to challenge them. Often this requires doing no more than two things – stating the assumptions out loud and then asking – "Why do we think this is true?"

Nadella's way of challenging the group schema that had ossified Microsoft into a technology corporation riding on its past successes was to return to asking the question about Microsoft's very purpose. He did that by evoking the past: the "what was." In his very first letter to every Microsoft employee, he wrote: "*Today is a very humbling day for me. It reminds me of my very first day at Microsoft, 22 years ago. Like you, I had a choice about where to come to work. I came here because I believed Microsoft was the best company in the world. I saw then how clearly we empower people to do magical things with our creations and ultimately make the world a better place. I knew there was no better company to join if I wanted to make a difference. This is the very same inspiration that continues to drive me today.*"[4]

But he knew the past was at loggerheads with the prevailing culture at Microsoft and Nadella surfaced that. In an interview with Herminia Ibarra,[5] Nadella revealed: "*Microsoft's culture had been rigid. Each employee had to prove to everyone that he or she was the smartest person in the room. Accountability – delivering on time and hitting numbers – trumped everything. Meetings were formal. If a senior leader wanted to tap the energy and creativity of someone lower down in the organisation, she or he needed to invite that person's boss, and so on. Hierarchy and pecking order had taken control, and spontaneity and creativity had suffered.*"

Nadella surfaced the fundamental assumption that being smart, accountable, and in control of resources were important to success. He asked "why?" challenging the idea that these assumptions would drive the future. When we step into the tide, our goal is disruption, changing the flow of the tide. Stepping into the stream is the beginning.

Embodying Ambitious Realism

Once you disrupt the flow of the tide, you can begin to shape it toward a more productive future, guiding *what is* toward *what can be*. If stepping into the tide helps disrupt the way those around you think about how the world works, the role of ambitious realism is to shape the way they act. Shaping the "way things are done" – our norms and our culture, is the necessary companion to disrupting the way we think.

Stories shape the norms – the culture – of those we lead. While this has always been the case, it is arguably even more important in a hybrid or a virtual work scenario. Let us give you an illustration. While we have no doubt that the following example has been told by many people in many places, we first heard it from Scott Snook at Harvard University and so will give him credit for it.

> *Imagine a gorilla in a large, tall cage. In the cage there is also a stool and hanging from the top of the cage are a bunch of bananas. Outside the cage are some social scientists with a hose. When the gorilla steps on the stool to get the bananas, the scientists turn the hose on him. Soon the gorilla learns not to step on the stool. Then the scientists introduce a new gorilla into the cage. When the new gorilla steps onto the stool to get the bananas (likely with a look of confusion as to why his cage mate is not doing so), the original gorilla, in fear of a hosing, beats the new gorilla. After a few attempts, and beatings, the second gorilla learns not to step on the stool. A third and fourth gorilla are introduced into the cage with similar results. Then – the original gorilla is removed, and a new gorilla is put into the cage. Of course, the other four dissuade him – aggressively – from stepping on the stool. We now have a group of gorillas, sitting in a cage with a bunch of bananas that they will not try to reach, and none of them could tell you why. A norm is formed: a culture set.*

Naturally, this model does not apply only to gorillas. In a landmark study of electric assembly workers in the 1930s, Fritz Roethlisberger[6] described the impact of socially developed and reinforced norms on productivity. Decades later, psychologist Albert Bandura[7] would become famous for discovering the process of social learning: learning from observing role models. Using these works as a foundation, leaders have been exhorted to "lead by example."

Fine, however, as historian Yuval Harari[8] points out, among the great leaps mankind made in our evolution to homo sapiens was our ability to tell stories. Leading by example allowed primates to shape the culture of those they could see, that is, the gorillas in their cage. Stories allow leaders to shape the norms and cultures of vast religions, of global movements, of nations, of organizations, of departments, all composed of followers whom the leader may never meet in person, may never get to personally direct, or to serve as a physically visible example. Rather, by creating and telling stories, leaders build not only a shared understanding of the world the followers face, but most importantly, the most effective responses to it.

Two Types of Stories

More than ever, in a virtual disconnected world, you must seek to build connection, engagement, and meaning through stories. You become visible through the stories you tell. Embodying ambitious realism requires you to tell two types of stories. One is a story about what is. You must create a shared narrative about what the tide looks like right now – that is the "realism" part, driven by the insights gleaned through the Humble Safari.

The "ambition" part of ambitious realism comes from telling stories about the future, what could be. These future-oriented stories help to create a shared narrative about how the tide *could* be shifted. They create a common conversation that allows aspiration to become strategy, then policy, then reality.

What do future-oriented stories look like? They can take many forms, but they contain some common elements including the fact that they are inclusive. As the great storyteller Andrew Stanton[9] taught us in his TED Talk, great stories are somewhat incomplete, and they make the listener care. These are both inclusionary demands. To make someone care about a story means that the story itself is relatable to their interests, needs, and concerns: it includes them. To make a story somewhat incomplete means inviting the listener to complete the story, to contribute, and help shape it, to include themselves in the story.

Inclusion in its truest sense is about engaging across a spectrum of views, perspectives, and life experiences in a way that brings voices both into the room and, importantly, together. Liz Wiseman[10] has called this being a "debate maker." We see inclusion as moving beyond a willingness to ask questions (though clearly this is important), to fostering a dialogue and demonstrating both an acceptance of novel approaches, and a demonstrable respect that differing life experiences have value. It is important to remember that inclusion is a felt emotion rather than a rational thought-construct. To feel included taps into one of the oldest emotional needs we carry as human beings: the need to belong. Because of the very nature of the social development of the human brain, the need to belong and to feel included remains a powerful indicator of performance, motivation, and well-being.

Perhaps most importantly, Stanton teaches us that stories must begin with the end in mind. If Stepping into the Tide involves creating a disruption, Embodying Ambitious Realism creates a potential new direction for the tide, a compelling way to respond to a narrative about how the world could look if the tide were set into a new path.

Let's return to the story of Nadella's efforts to transform Microsoft. Once he had stepped into the tide and disrupted the way the people of Microsoft thought about the tide, he set about changing the narrative about how they would shape it. According to Herminia Ibarra, at Microsoft's July 2015 global sales conference in Orlando, Nadella revealed a fresh company mission: *"To empower every person and every organisation on the planet to achieve more."* The original mission enshrined by Gates was *"a computer on every desk and in every home."* As Ibarra writes, *"Nadella's to-do list for the first year included preparing Microsoft for a mobile- and cloud-first world, building 'new and surprising partnerships' and working to ensure they could truly empower every person on the planet as their new mission stated."*

The new story helped transform Microsoft's strategy and culture. They were able to let go of Nokia mobile phones, they acquired LinkedIn, they transformed the relationship with Minecraft and Activision Blizzard, and expanded their cloud business Azure. The stock that had been flat for 14 years would eventually grow 9 times to a valuation which places Microsoft as the world's most valuable company.

The Talent Challenge

Creating a disruption in the flow of the tide by stepping into it and creating a new understanding is the first step. Next is to set a new way of acting within the tide to shift its flow toward an inclusive story of what could be. Remember, this will only work if you and your organization have the skills to execute. Here, in the Talent Challenge, you will find the most difficult aspect of the practice of Adaptive Impact: shaping your capabilities and those of your organization to build a dynamic culture of developmental curiosity and growth.

In the past, leaders and organizations have tried to simplify this task by creating static development targets: lists of skills and capabilities to acquire. Taking a moment to reflect on the fact that your efforts to shape the future are embedded in a constantly flowing, changing tide makes the idea of a static list of skills or competencies seem antithetical. Rather, the focus on building talent must be approached with the same humility as the humble safari, through constant, open questioning and a comfort with uncertainty. The Talent Challenge needs to be approached with what we refer to as Dynamic Curiosity and Curating Capabilities.

Dynamic Curiosity

"Dynamic Curiosity" is a term made famous by Satya Nadella based on the concept of "Growth Mindset" outlined in Carol Dweck's best-selling book: *Mindset: The New Psychology of Success.* Let's return to the story of the turn-around Satya Nadella led at Microsoft. During that same speech at Microsoft's July 2015 global sales conference, Nadella said, "*...culture is not a static thing. It is about a dynamic learning culture. In fact, the phrase we use to describe our emerging culture is 'growth mindset,' because it's about every individual, every one of us having that attitude – that mindset – of being able to overcome any constraint, stand up to any challenge, making it possible for us to grow and thereby for the company to grow.*"

Developing a culture of Dynamic Curiosity is an immense leadership challenge. In practice, it means that you must challenge the organization's need for certainty and the individuals' default system of going into autopilot mode. However, the ability to remain in a continuous state of curiosity and seek root causes has been central to and embedded in leadership approaches as diverse as the Five-Whys of LEAN, and the Agile Manifesto. Your task in creating Dynamic Curiosity is to help others and yourself become comfortable with uncertainty and remain constantly curious, always asking what different demands the future will impose. Dynamic curiosity helps you and the organization move quickly by fostering continuous learning and a willingness to let go of the irrelevant. Of course, understanding the demands that are coming is one thing, being prepared to deliver on these demands is another: enter the idea of Curating Capabilities.

Curating Capabilities

Curating Capabilities refers to your ability to constantly scan and compare the demands of the environment to your and your organization's own strengths and to continually refine the list of needed skills, then doing the work to develop them. The goal of Curating Capabilities is to continually ensure relevance and to find paths to combine the potential human and automated work, even at the task level. This stands in stark contrast to the more common practice of building skill inventories or "competency models." Think of competency models as a balance sheet. These models give you a picture of a point in time, useful for a moment. Instead of building highly refined pictures of a single point in time, curating capabilities means to continually refine your understanding of the skills you (or your organization) need.

By definition, an environment subject to continuous change belies the ability to define a set of skills that will carry an individual to success over time. Recognizing this, yet still searching for a definitive list of teachable skills, some have turned to the concept of Learning Agility. While we believe that the idea of Learning Agility or, as Vivienne Ming,[11] founder of the think tank Socos, calls it, "Meta Learning," is important, we are still left with an obvious, yet uncomfortable truth: there are skills to master, but no skill set to master. Leadership agency means accepting the responsibility to constantly, and uniquely, curate the list of skills you need, assess yourself against this list, work to gain the skills, and then start all over again. It defines and supports the essential cycle for you and those you lead to grow their skills: Curate. Assess. Master. Re-curate ... The task is never complete.

We have three pieces of advice to help in building well-curated capabilities. First, willingly seek assistance in assessing your abilities and mastering skills. Second, do not seek packaged lists of skills to build; you must do this yourself. As you build this list, remember the zoom lens! Zoom in to see the skills you need to drive your immediate accountabilities and zoom out to see the skills you will need tomorrow. Finally, don't forget that you are never done. Continuing this process is the key.

We noted at the start of the chapter that not delivering on the practice of Adaptive Impact leaves you "Stuck in Neutral," a state of continual, incremental improvement against present challenges based on past assumptions. Now that we have some insight into the practice of Adaptive Impact, let's look at two contrasting examples, two different Maria Moments that will illustrate the difference between leading while being Stuck in Neutral versus leading with Adaptive Impact.

TWO MARIA MOMENTS

Stuck in Neutral

Maria had a college buddy who worked at an old-line industrial firm. Seventy-five years earlier, the company's lionized founder had taken the business, which had been successful at the time, and bet the organization's future on an emerging technology. The bet paid off and the company became the leader in its field. At the time Maria's friend joined, another emerging technology was making its way onto the scene. This time, the current CEO was hesitant. He did what so many late-20th-century mindset leaders had learned to do; he established a small division to explore and grow the new technology while exhorting the rest of the company to capitalize on their market leader position with their current products. In quiet private meetings, all of the younger, newer managers and leaders complained about the company's timidity and predicted its long-term demise as they remained stuck, beholden to their current success. Maria had more than one drink listening to her friend complain about being trapped by success.
    Compared to...

Adaptive Impact

Early in her career, Maria worked in financial services in a very old, very large, and extremely successful global firm. Her first observation was that the average tenure of the employees was about 20+ years. Maria looked around and thought, I can learn the basics here, but this place is going nowhere. *And then, she was surprised. First, the leadership of the organization reset their view of the competition and announced that they considered themselves to be competitors in the FinTech world, though they were badly behind. They were not, as the rest of the world saw them, leaders in traditional finance. Second,*

> *the company started to make acquisitions and divestitures – some that worked, some that failed – to change the business mix. Third, they announced a generous early retirement program and it was made clear that this would be followed by a reduction in force. One-third of the employees left, new staff were hired in key roles, and the average tenure was cut in half. Maria looked around and thought,* This place is actually thinking about sustaining success into the future, not resting on its successful past.

IN SUMMARY

And so, what is Adaptive Impact? Is it a goal, an objective, a state of mind, a capability? What does it feel like when it has been achieved? How does one stay in this zone of leadership agency? In short, Adaptive Impact is focused action. Action directed at gaining results-beyond-results. This is made possible through your efforts to create for yourself and your constituents the broadest freedom to act toward a shared view of the future, while continually redefining that future and building the capabilities to succeed. Living in a state of Adaptive Impact will inevitably leave you feeling unfinished, unfulfilled, and hungry, but in a good way. It is always a work in progress, much like Thomas Jefferson's idea of forming "a more perfect union." It is successful but never finished, always striving.

Here are the key concepts we discussed in this chapter (Figure 5.4).

"That's unusual for you, a PowerPoint presentation with just a few slides and only a few words," grinned Frida Kahlo as she peeked over Maria Miller's shoulder as Maria finished up her prep for her department staff meeting. It had been six months since Maria received the poor results from the first Employee Engagement Survey after she and John had made changes to the department.

Well, it's been an interesting period, *Maria thought in response. Maria had spent the last six months meeting not only with her team but with as many of the stakeholders of her team as she could, just learning.* "We had made a lot of changes, but I'm not sure I ever considered how to make them sustainable. I need to get the team to think differently and more importantly, get them personally involved in what tomorrow could be like," said *Maria over her shoulder to Frida's fading image.*

ADAPTIVE IMPACT	
Leading the organization, team, and one's self forward in a way that creates sustainable success and on-going relevance.	
CONCEPT SUMMARY	
Stepping into the Tide	Locating the critical pivot point where the ever-changing stream of business systems, technology, societal demands, consumer trends and competitor activity meet and creating a meaningful disruption to shape the flow.
Humble Safari	Reaching out and learning about the organization beyond your formal accountabilities.
Challenging the Assumptive Schema	Asking the difficult questions to surface underlying assumptions and testing the "why" that drives the current ways of working.
Embodying Ambitious Realism	Shaping the way the organization acts, i.e. the ways of working, norms and culture through inclusive storytelling.
Storytelling	The narrative that leaders create about what the tide looks like right now and about what the future could be. A common conversation that allows aspiration to become strategy, then policy, then reality.
Inclusion	Engaging across a spectrum of views, perspectives, and life experience in a way that brings voices both into the room and together.
Meeting the Talent Challenge	Ensuring that you and those others around you remain continually relevant to meet the challenges on the horizon through Dynamic Curiosity and Curating Capabilities.
Dynamic Curiosity	Remaining in a constant state of incompletion, accomplished by shifting perspectives from "know" it all to "learn" it all.
Curating Capabilities	Constantly scanning and comparing the demands of the environment to one's own strengths in order to continually refine the list of requisite skills – then doing the work to develop those skills.

FIGURE 5.4
Adaptive Impact Concept Summary

NOTES

1 *The Legend of Bagger Vance*, Feature Film, dir. Robert Redford (DreamWorks, 2000).
2 Steven Pressfield, *The Legend of Bagger Vance: A Novel of Golf and the Game of Life* (London: Bantam Books, 2021).

3 Herminia Ibarra, Aneeta Rattan, and Anna Johnston, "Satya Nadella at Microsoft: Instilling a Growth Mindset," Case Study (London Business School, June 1, 2008), https://hbsp.harvard.edu/product/LBS128-PDF-ENG.

4 Ibarra, Rattan, and Johnston.

5 Ibarra, Rattan, and Johnston.

6 Fritz J. Roethlisberger and William J. Dickson, *Management and the Worker: An Account of a Research Program Conducted by the Western Electric Company, Hawthorne Works, Chicago*, 17th printing (Cambridge, Mass.: Harvard Univ. Press, 1976).

7 Albert Bandura, "Social Learning through Imitation," in *Nebraska Symposium on Motivation*, ed. M.R. Jones (Lincoln, NE: University of Nebraska Press, 1962), 211–74.

8 Yuval N. Harari, *Sapiens: A Brief History of Humankind*, First U.S. edition (New York: Harper, 2015).

9 *The Clues to a Great Story*, TED Talk, 2012, https://www.ted.com/talks/andrew_stanton_the_clues_to_a_great_story.

10 Liz Wiseman, *Multipliers: How the Best Leaders Make Everyone Smarter*, Revised and updated edition (New York: Harper Business, 2017).

11 Sudhanshu Palsule and Michael Chavez, *Rehumanizing Leadership: Putting Purpose Back into Business* (Madrid: LID, 2020).

6

The Paradox of Developing Leadership Agency: Step Back, Let Go, Step Forward

WHERE MARIA LEARNS FROM HER HORRIBLE, NO GOOD, VERY FORTUNATE DAY

"Just put that box in the corner," Maria Miller said to the mover. The office was still taking shape. She had selected a comfortable space with some room to grow on Holles St. in London's Soho area; her office had a great view of Cavendish Square Garden.

"Here you go," said Bobby walking into Maria's still unpacked office and handing her a coffee. "Tara, Mike, and Bill will be here in 30 minutes, and we can get our first official meeting started." Bobby hustled off and started to call out to the IT guy who was setting up their network and servers. Maria was glad everyone would be together to get things off the ground.

The new boss sat back in her chair, sipped her coffee, and smiled. "You've had that smile on your face for three weeks straight now," said the voice of Frida Kahlo, whom Maria imagined was perched on a stack of unpacked boxes.

Sure have, though it was a tough road to find it, *thought Maria.*

"Yes, I remember the day well," said Frida, as she took Maria back to one of the hardest days in her professional life.

It was a little after 3:00 when Maria received a call from Ted Markus, Percipience Ltd.'s lead director and chair of the governance committee,

DOI: 10.4324/9781003491880-6

asking her to dinner. For six months the trade press had been blogging rumors that Percipience Ltd.'s CEO, Jake Faddle, was going to retire. While the company refused to comment on the rumors, Jake announced in a staff meeting three months later that he would be leaving at the end of the year. No one in the room leaked a word but within weeks, Board members were starting to take meetings with the likely candidates to replace Jake. Astute lieutenants and assistants were quick to catch on and soon the company was buzzing.

Maria was one of three internal candidates who had obviously been groomed for the role over the previous two years. The savvy scuttlebutt was that the Board was also looking at one outsider. Maria had met over drinks, lunch, or in the office with most of the Board over the past two months and her stomach did a flip when she got the call from Ted. I've worked hard. I'm ready, she remembered thinking as she hung up the phone.

Three hours later, she arrived at the quiet and rather expensive restaurant Ted had chosen. She was 10 minutes early, but Ted was already there. She sat, smiled, and ordered a drink. Maria had always admired Ted. He was a mix of graciousness and deadly serious. Every discussion they'd had was to the point but was also a positive experience. Drinks arrived while they exchanged pleasantries. Once the server left, Ted looked at Maria and said quietly, "Let me get to the point. This afternoon the Board offered the CEO job to Charles Yang." Ted paused to give Maria space to absorb the news.

"Maria, you are terrific. The Board had no doubt, in fact, that you were the best person to lead us to outstanding performance over the next five years." Ted said this as a fact, not a verbal arm around the shoulder designed to soften the blow. "But here's the thing," he continued. "As you met and talked to Board members about the future of the company, there were no surprises, nothing outside the norm. Frankly, Maria, you were seen as an exceptional caretaker – not someone who would lead us to our next incarnation."

"I know that's a bit harsh," Ted continued, "but it speaks to the depth of impact you have had at Percipience Ltd. already. The company has your fingerprints all over it – in a good way. You should be proud," encouraged Ted. "In fact, Charles told us one of his first steps would be to appoint you Chief Operating Officer and put a substantial part of the business under you. We all hope you will be part of our future at the company."

The rest of the evening was a blur that Maria barely remembered. The next morning, she headed off to the gym for a tough workout and then visited the steam room. She said out loud to the empty space, *"Sure, sit there in that floral dress, you're not real anyway."*

"Don't take your disappointment out on me," said the image of Frida Kahlo in Maria's mind, undisturbed by the steam and heat. *"Ted's right, you know."*

Drawing her attention back to the present day and the unpacked office, Kahlo asked, "Do you remember the rest of our discussion that day?"

I do, *thought Maria.* It took some time and a difficult look in the mirror, but the truth was I had built a great team and a great organization, and they were ready to fly – I was in the way. If I stayed, it would have been bad for all of us. I really needed to re-invent myself, find a new purpose.

"As I told you," said Frida, standing up and fading from Maria's mind, *"step back, let go, and step forward into something new."*

"It's time!" Bobby called from down the hall.

"Coming!" replied Maria, getting out of her chair, still smiling.

Perhaps this episode of Maria's journey left you surprised or dissatisfied. Unfortunately, there is no neat and tidy narrative when it comes to leadership development; it is necessarily a meandering journey of discovery, insight, and increasing self-awareness. It is a path that requires an understanding of the themes of paradox and perspective. As Maria experienced, it is possible to be hopeful and learn from pain. And equally as important, you can achieve success yet still be unfinished.

THE PARADOX OF LEARNING HOW TO GUIDE THE TIDE

The development of leaders is – and has been for some time – largely based on guided experiences driven by individual career ambition, a hunger for achievement, the exercise of power, and seeking recognition by upward movement through the hierarchy. This is unlikely to change, nor should it. Impactful, meaningful experiences, thoughtfully guided, and paired with a complementary focus on improving personal capabilities have proven to be a successful foundation of human development. However, the development of practices to guide the tide requires additional and often a profoundly different set of underlying dynamics than what have been traditionally utilized in leadership development. Let us examine the key ones here.

The Need to Achieve Perspective

"How do I achieve the best possible impact in the world around me?" To answer this question requires a perspective – a vantage point – from where to observe and understand yourself and your interaction with the world. How can you position yourself to observe yourself, both your leadership impact and your growth as a leader? How can you best achieve that perspective? The answer is to pull yourself out of the immediate situation, to step up onto the "balcony." As Heifetz and Linsky outlined in their "Survival Guide for Leaders"[1]:

> *The ability to maintain perspective in the midst of action is critical to lowering resistance. Any military officer knows the importance of maintaining the capacity for reflection, especially in the "fog of war." Great athletes must simultaneously play the game and observe it as a whole. We call this skill "getting off the dance floor and going to the balcony," an image that captures the mental activity of stepping back from the action and asking, "What's really going on here?"*

Obtaining the required perspective can seem impossible when you are so clearly the protagonist in your own development story. *Guiding the tide* is based on transforming your leadership approach when it comes to impacting others. The problem is that the ambition necessary to draw the lessons and skills of leadership from significant, powerful experiences (and perhaps some coaching) can also adversely lead us back to Inertia. The core paradox of the journey is that someone who is successful in guiding the tide risks becoming inert again. They end up turning their sense of purpose into iconic status – frozen and limiting – where Adaptive Impact, the ability to address reality, and Honest Engagement devolve into being stuck in neutral, certitude, and trading away values to maintain status. This is a familiar parable we have all seen too many times. The satisfaction that comes from being a successful leader in the eyes of others leads to forgetting what led to success in the first place, and so turns into a story of hubris and failure.

The only alternative is to actively and continuously create a **cycle of renewal**. Building leadership Agency takes mindful ongoing effort to draw productive lessons from life experiences – focused on the practices described in prior chapters. But this is not enough. Once you have reached a place of success and comfort, it is time to force yourself to begin the

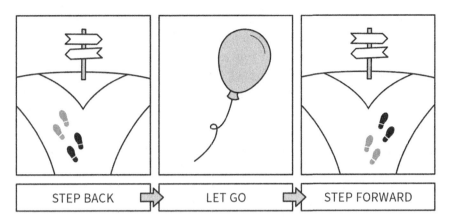

FIGURE 6.1
Renewal Cycle

development cycle again. In other words, get comfortable being uncomfortable. Periodically you will need to practice the virtuous learning loop of Stepping Back, Letting Go, and Stepping Forward (Figure 6.1).

Let's examine each one of them in some detail.

Step Back – the Attraction of Balconies

Remember Heifetz' balcony analogy? The best leaders we've seen can step back from their leadership roles to take stock and observe themselves and the ways in which they lead. These leaders have learned how to put themselves regularly and systematically "*on the balcony*" and have built the wisdom of knowing what to look for and how to make sense out of what they observe. This leaves us with two questions: "*When do I step up to the balcony?*" and "*What do I look for?*"

The answer to the first question is straightforward though not specific: step up to the balcony periodically. For most of us this means setting up "reflection" times which can be quarterly, annually, when major projects are drawing to a close, or a new project is about to begin. An analogy to sailing is in order here. When the wind starts to pick up and the sailboat is moving fast, sailors may shorten sail (called reefing) to keep the boat in control. Deciding when to reef is always a judgment call but the old adage is, "*The time to reef is as soon as you start to wonder if you should think about reefing.*" The same is true of reflection. If you can't recall the last time you stepped up to the balcony, it is time to do so. If you are wondering if it is a good time to pause and reflect, then it most certainly is. If things are going very smoothly, it's time to step back.

The second question – what I should be looking for? – is a bit more involved. For this, we need to go back to what successfully guiding the tide looks like. We have described the goal of leadership agency as the ability to guide the tide in order to deliver results-beyond-results: achieving targeted goals while delivering meaningful impacts on followership, sustainability, and Humanocity in the workplace. When you step up to the balcony, use each component of these outcomes of guiding the tide to assess your progress:

Followership
- Does my team trust each other?
- Do we have a unified direction?
- Are we attracting talent?
- Do people on my team feel safe to take risks and express themselves?

Sustainability
- Do we focus our energy on goals that make a difference?
- Are we balancing long- and short-term well?
- Are we delivering more value than we consume?
- Can everyone see the big picture – do we connect the dots?

Humanocity
- Do others see me as a role model?
- Does everyone on the team have a meaningful way to contribute?
- Are we building a competitive advantage?
- Is our strategy driven by a clear purpose – do we know our "Why"?

Being on the balcony is difficult. While you will need to spend some time there alone, feel free to bring along some friends. You can do this in the form of trusted mentors or coaches, those who will honestly share their perspective rather than simply become an echo chamber for your thoughts. You can seek input from your team either through informal conversations or through more formal mechanisms such as employee surveys, customer data, formal coaching, or 360° feedback. But here is the truly difficult part: when the answer to most of these questions is yes, and you are doing well, it's time for you to LET GO.

Let Go – How Did It Get So Late So Soon?

Everything is going well. You've built a great organization/team/process and the view from the balcony is wonderful ... so it's time to let go. This can happen so much more quickly than we expect, or want. Moving from a place of success and comfort to an arena where we need to build something new is difficult and challenging. It is also necessary if you and the organization you have built are to avoid stagnation. Let us be very clear: what we are talking about here is NOT the next promotion, or taking on a more senior role in your same area of accountability. Letting go means finding a new tide, a new set of followers, newly refocused purpose, and a different set of challenges within which to create sustainable success, and new constituents for whom a humanized context can be developed.

Letting Go comes with three core challenges: handing-off effectively, becoming comfortable with discomfort, and self-care. Let us take a look at each in turn.

Handing-off Effectively

The parable of Maria's journey is useful to return to here. It took a career's worth of experiences for Maria to find out which of her ambitions were legitimately and appropriately hers, and the ones that were best left to others. When the Percipience Ltd. Board passed her over for the CEO role, she was forced to confront the idea that she needed to move on. As she debriefed with Frida on her deeply disruptive decision to leave Percipience Ltd., she reflected on the fact that it also helped her to learn to see things as they are rather than to be blinded by her own certitude. It is this sense of comfort with change and a level of self-worth that allowed Maria to process this experience so constructively. Maria, with some difficulty, became comfortable with the fact that others may have been more suitable for some roles and tasks than she was. Imagine what would have happened had she chosen to stay with Percipience Ltd. as their new COO or even if the Board had offered her the CEO role. Would she have grown enough? Would the organization have continued to innovate? Or would they have just kept repeating past successes until it became failure?

The trap for a leader when letting go is focusing on "continuity". This means working to ensure that those to whom you entrust your legacy will maintain fidelity to what you have built. This is the road to stagnation.

Alternatively, letting go productively requires you to focus on ensuring that your successors have the capacity to guide the tide themselves rather than the ability to maintain your legacy. They cannot simply be you; they must be free to forge their own path, to develop their own unique sense of agency. Ask yourself, have you created a legacy of agency? How have you:

- Built the practices within your team for Honest Engagement? Do they have real conversations even when difficult? Is the team connected to its values? Does it have purpose?
- Established the tools and mechanisms for Addressing Reality? Does the team think from a systems perspective, and have passion grounded in realism? Are they inclusive, risk taking, and do they show empathy?
- Created the capacity for Adaptive Impact? Does the team continually step into the tide to test and disrupt their thinking? Do they build inclusive stories about what the future can become and are they relentlessly curious about what they will need to succeed? Do they appreciate the benefits and possibilities of the integration of human creativity with technology?

This is the real work and responsibility of building succession, which goes well beyond the box-filling of traditional continuity plans. It's about ensuring that the leaders who follow you are ready to lead, rather than ready to preserve your legacy. Supporting others in their efforts to build leadership agency is a challenge in and of itself. However, the biggest challenge of Letting Go is actually moving on to something new.

Stepping Forward – Next Please

I will take with me the emptiness of my hands
What you do not have you find everywhere

W.S. Merwin

So, what's next? How do you step into a new set of circumstances, a new "tide" that will allow you to continue to lead with agency? Ed Schein explains that while the immediate circumstances in life may pull us one way or another, much like a boat at anchor, our most central values will always pull us back to careers and work that is consistent with those values.[2] Other authors have focused on our capabilities as the drivers that set us on a path. Some others have talked about seeking to make a positive contribution to the world. It's helpful to consider the simplified quote often attributed to Mahatma Gandhi, "Be the Change you want to see in the world." However, this idea is drawn from something much more thoughtful and relevant that Gandhi wrote in a 1913 journal article for *Indian Opinion*:[3]

> We but mirror the world. All the tendencies present in the outer world are to be found in the world of our body. If we could change ourselves, the tendencies in the world would also change. As a man changes his own nature, so does the attitude of the world change towards him. This is the divine mystery supreme. A wonderful thing it is and the source of our happiness. We need not wait to see what others do.

We believe that all three of these perspectives – values, activities, and social impact – have merit. As you look to the future, consider the intersection of these three circles in a classic Venn diagram. In one circle, list your most closely held values. In a second, list the activities that you most enjoy doing (even if you're not yet excellent at them). Finally, in the third circle, list the ways you would like to impact the world around you (Figure 6.2).

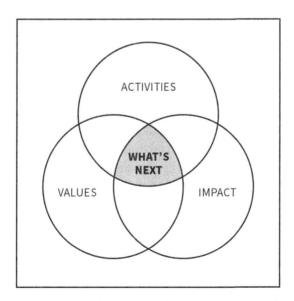

FIGURE 6.2
Stepping Forward

As you review opportunities and consider options, use these three circles as your measurement standard: your personal evaluation lens. When you find the opportunity that fits the intersection of these three considerations, you've found what is next for you. Please notice the verb we've used in that last sentence: find. That is not an accident. The imperative of leadership development is there not only when we are leading others but also when we lead ourselves. We will discuss the mechanics of developing yourself in the next chapter. However, for right now, let's take a moment to point out the obvious. Stepping into something new, even when you find that opportunity that lies at the heart of your values, interests, and hoped-for impact, is uncomfortable. Being willing to put yourself into uncomfortable situations and then dealing productively with discomfort is critical to Stepping Forward.

Comfort with Discomfort

Moving on to something new is hard. Letting go of the familiar, leaving an arena in which we have been successful, and stepping into something you cannot fully predict creates a lot of discomfort. The challenge with discomfort is, of course, that it is stressful. In situations where the stakes are high, you will find that uncertainty reigns supreme and you will be scrutinized and judged by others for signs of stress.[4] When we leave the familiar and move on to something new, we inevitably create loss; we lose relationships, a sense of competence, security, ownership, and the familiarity of the norms to which we have become accustomed.

Dealing with these stressors, counter intuitively, does not mean avoiding them. Stressors are inevitable.[5] Fortunately, researchers have identified strategies to cope with stress while it occurs.[6] Coping mechanisms include venting about the situation, seeking the support of others, and planning to address the cause(s) of stress. Other researchers have focused on recovering from stress – that is returning to the level of functioning you experienced before the stress.[7] Most often this involves detaching yourself psychologically from the source of the stress. In other words, taking a break. Creating periodic distance from work and career challenges, setting them aside for a bit, and focusing on a different activity can help tremendously in recovering from stress.

All of these are valuable approaches for day-to-day stressors. But more is needed as part of the process of Letting Go. What is called for here is what many researchers refer to as "renewal"[8] or "post-traumatic growth."[9] Unlike coping or recovery, renewal is a process that focuses on becoming *more*: more able to be creative and handle complexity, more open to new experiences, improved ability to build relationships, deeper appreciation for life, and an increased sense of purpose. How do we turn stressful, even traumatic experiences into an opportunity for renewal? Many researchers have studied this question and from their work we draw four recommendations:

First, don't go it alone. Find your own Frida! Having a support system is important. Just as Maria "found" Frida, you can seek out trusted advisors and/or colleagues, even to the point of creating an informal and personal "board of directors" to whom you can reach out and test your understanding and response to situations. Perhaps you can use professional coaches, family members, mentors, or even spiritual guides. The most important thing is to have others to help, share ideas, and listen to you. Choose people who can help broaden and challenge your perspective and offer both practical and emotional support as you let go and transition to something new.

Second, reset your "assumptive schema." Psychologists define assumptive schema as our fundamental assumptions about how the world works. Do we assume that people are generally good, altruistic, selfish, demanding, etc.? Do we trust that things balance out over time, or do we need to be sure each transaction itself is fair? Are we operating on an island with our actions independent of the world around us, or do we see vast interconnections – and if so – what are they? Letting go of familiar roles and patterns of success challenges us to rethink our assumptions about how the world works. Taking the time to surface your assumptions, examine them critically, and thoughtfully choose which assumptions to bring with you and which to rethink.

Third, tell your story. All our lives are stories. Living and leading with agency in large part means being the author of your story rather than simply being a character driven along by the plot. Letting go of your present successful situation in order to step into something new provides a great temptation to allow circumstances to drive you. Avoid this temptation. Write the story of your future. Where are you going? Why? What will you try to achieve? What prompted the change? Once you know the answers to these questions, tell your story to others. This act or creating and then telling your own story has been shown to have a powerful impact on our ability to turn stressful experiences into growth experiences.[10,11]

<u>Fourth, have the confidence in your ability to grow.</u> Stressful experiences can, in and of themselves, have a tremendous impact on your ability to grow. Nothing breeds confidence like experience. The more often you are willing to step into something new, the more experience you have being open to experience, the more likely you are to see your confidence increase. In fact, in a meta-analysis of 26 large studies of post-traumatic experiences, researchers found that more than half of all people will experience growth as a result of deeply trying circumstances.[12]

Self-Care

Finally, it is important to recognize that letting go takes energy and resilience. Making self-care a priority is critical for leaders to be able to successfully Let Go. Successful leaders make their own resilience a non-negotiable for the way they lead; they role-model this approach to those they lead. Self-care is not a trite buzzword, it's a necessary concept. Without the implementation of self-care, none of the other recommendations will survive over the course of a career.

Fortunately, there are a multitude of resources available today that can help to address the need for self-care. While we will not take the time to review all of these approaches, you may wish to check out the approach Tony Schwartz takes in his book *The Way We Are Working Isn't Working.*[13] In it, Schwartz identifies and discusses four categories or "pillars" of energy capacity required to power sustainable peak performance:

- Physical energy – the need for bodily health, how we manage our fitness and lifestyle.
- Emotional energy – the need for security; how we feel accepted and valued.
- Mental energy – the need for self-expression; realizing our innate desire to express ourselves effectively by controlling our attention and focus.
- Spiritual energy – the need for significance, meaning, and connection, recognizing that we serve something bigger than ourselves.

In the End – There Is No Escaping Joseph Campbell

Joseph Campbell[14] studied all of the notable myths, legends, and stories that humans have told themselves from Gilgamesh to Luke Skywalker. He found a repeating pattern in their stories that he called *The Hero's Journey*. Without summarizing his exhaustive body of work here, suffice it to say that Campbell found that the protagonist in all of our stories – the hero, the leader – follows a consistent pattern in their growth and development:

1. Their existing, stable world changes (Odysseus goes to war, Peter Parker is bitten by a radioactive spider, and Bruce Wayne's parents die.)
2. Their new adventure is filled with challenging experiences, helpers, and, at times, failure, all of which bring both new skills and a deeper understanding of themselves (Hercules finds his way past the 12 challenges, Darth Vader turns out to be Luke's father, and Macbeth is tortured by the decision to kill Duncan.)
3. Their new skills and awareness allow them to bring about a new, deeper level of success (Arthur creates the Knights of the Round Table, Gandalf guides the Fellowship to defeat Sauron, and Dorothy teams with the others to find the Wizard of Oz.)
4. The cycle begins again.

In essence, this is similar to the pattern we have been discussing – with one big exception. As Campbell describes it, each cycle in *The Hero's Journey* is kick-started by an external event. Certainly, this will be true in your journey to Guiding the Tide. Externally driven challenging experiences, sometimes called crucibles, are critical learning experiences and challenges that need to be productively addressed and from which we derive critical lessons.

While these externally driven experiences are irreplaceable development opportunities, successfully maintaining momentum also means pursuing something that sounds counterintuitive: creating your own crucibles. Certainly, this is not simple or easy and is not something that will happen often. It requires fortitude and intent – a willingness to take a risk and step into something new – of your own volition.

However, this is the driving principle behind Step Back–Let Go–Step Forward. Moving and learning through your own "Hero's Journey" is critical for development. Restarting the cycle does not have to be – in fact should *not* be – an externally driven event. You are not Bilbo Baggins, content to stay in your Hobbit hole reading and eating until forced out of it by Gandalf. Seizing control of your own story by stepping back, letting go, and stepping forward to something new will ensure both you – and the organization you have built – avoid inertia.

IN SUMMARY

Be your own author. As we close out this chapter, it is useful to restate the obvious; agency requires you to embrace your own future. Passively waiting for an opportunity that fits your personal lens to arrive is a strategy that makes you a character in your story rather than being the author. Seek out – or create – these opportunities. Be your own author. Write your own story.

In this chapter we have tried to show you how to activate what we call the cycle of renewal – stepping back – letting go – and stepping forward into something new. Again, we have introduced some new concepts and reframed some of the concepts we have introduced in prior chapters, all focused on taking control of your own hero's journey. Inevitably, your journey will include many (or at least some) deeply meaningful experiences, some difficult and some exhilarating, but all will be opportunities for growth. In the next chapter we will focus on *how* you can grow from these seminal experiences. In Figure 6.3 below we provide a chart summarizing the key new concepts in this chapter, the cycle of renewal, along with the key concepts that will be introduced in the next chapter.

As Maria sat down in the conference room surrounded by her new team, she looked up at the one decorating suggestion she'd made for the office; a print of the famous Frida Kahlo painting, "The Frame." It took her right back to that day in Paris when she first saw the painting and began to take a more active role in writing her own story.

She thought about leaving the world of finance for cloud computing. She thought about leaving the United States and moving to London. She even thought about leaving the world of multimedia to join Percipience Ltd. And now, she was leaving Percipience Ltd. to start her next journey. She considered all of the lessons she'd learned along the way. Well, Frida, *she thought as she looked at the painting,* it's been sometimes on purpose and sometimes by accident, but my career has been a cycle of stepping back, letting go, and stepping forward. I've been deeply inspired by how you wrote your own story. Here's hoping I keep writing mine.

Maria smiled at the team and began the meeting.

DEVELOPING LEADERSHIP AGENCY
Making the conscious choice to approach your life's experiences with purposeful intent to extract growth and wisdom, the ambition to create and learn from meaningful experiences for yourself, and the courage to continually renew yourself.

CONCEPT SUMMARY

Cycle of Renewal	Stepping Back to reflect and gain perspective, Letting Go of your place of success and comfort, and Stepping Forward to an arena where we need to build something new and find your "next."
The Bounce	Growth that is experienced from undergoing significant stressful life events – either positive or negative – is accomplished by re-setting your world view, seeking support from others, and telling your own story.
Simultaneity	Reckoning with paradoxical ideas by holding two different beliefs concurrently.
Reframe & Apply	Taking the insights you've gained from one seminal experience and discovering ways to apply these learnings across many varied situations. This is driven by narrative development – building a story of the future, and by seeking ways of being of service to others.

FIGURE 6.3
Developing Leadership Agency Concept Summary

NOTES

1 Ronald A. Heifetz and Marty Linsky, "A Survival Guide for Leaders," *Harvard Business Review*, June 2002, https://hbr.org/2002/06/a-survival-guide-for-leaders.

2 Edgar H. Schein, *Career Anchors: Discovering Your Real Values*, Rev. ed. (Amsterdam: Pfeiffer & Co., 1993).

3 The collected works of Mahatma Gandhi Vol. 13. https://www.gandhiashramsevagram.org/gandhi-literature/collected-works-of-mahatma-gandhi-volume-1-to-98.php.

4 Richard E. Boyatzis, D. Goleman, U. Dhar, and J.K. Osiri, "Thrive and Survive: Assessing Personal Sustainability," *Consulting Psychology Journal: Practice and Research* 73, no. 1 (March 2021): 27–50, https://doi.org/10.1037/cpb0000193.

5 Only 7% of Americans reported that they were able to identify effective strategies to reduce stress according to: Sophia Bethune and Angel Brownawell, "Americans Report Willpower and Stress as Key Obstacles to Meeting Health-Related Resolutions," Press Release (Washington: American Psychological Association, March 2010), https://www.apa.org/news/press/releases/2010/03/lifestyle-changes.

6 Susan Roth and Lawrence J. Cohen, "Approach, Avoidance, and Coping with Stress," *American Psychologist* 41, no. 7 (1986): 813–19, https://doi.org/10.1037/0003-066X.41.7.813.

7 Sabine Sonnentag and Charlotte Fritz, "Recovery from Job Stress: The Stressor-Detachment Model as an Integrative Framework: THE STRESSOR-DETACHMENT MODEL," *Journal of Organizational Behavior* 36, no. S1 (February 2015): S72–103, https://doi.org/10.1002/job.1924.

8 Boyatzis et al., "Thrive and Survive."

9 Richard G. Tedeschi and Lawrence G. Calhoun, "Posttraumatic Growth: Conceptual Foundations and Empirical Evidence," *Psychological Inquiry* 15, no. 1 (January 2004): 1–18, https://doi.org/10.1207/s15327965pli1501_01.

10 Tedeschi and Calhoun, "Posttraumatic Growth".

11 Nathan A. Bowling and Jeremy A. Schumm, "The COVID-19 Pandemic: A Source of Posttraumatic Growth?" *Industrial and Organizational Psychology* 14, nos 1–2 (June 2021): 184–88, https://doi.org/10.1017/iop.2021.31.

12 Xiaoli Wu A.C. Kaminga, W. Dai, J. Deng, Z. Wang, X Pan, and A. Liu, "The Prevalence of Moderate-to-High Posttraumatic Growth: A Systematic Review and Meta-Analysis," *Journal of Affective Disorders* 243 (January 2019): 408–15, https://doi.org/10.1016/j.jad.2018.09.023.

13 Tony Schwartz, *The Way We're Working Isn't Working: The Four Forgotten Needs That Energize Great Performance* (New York: Free Press, 2011).

14 Joseph Campbell, *The Hero with a Thousand Faces*, 3rd ed, Bollingen Series XVII (Novato, Calif: New World Library, 2008).

7

A Playbook for Leaders Developing Themselves

WHERE MARIA LEARNS TO TELL HER STORY

Maria absentmindedly pushed her cheek against the cool window of her limo as she headed through London on her way to the annual W³ (Women Who Win) Summit, where she was being given an award. "You seem distracted," said the voice of Frida Khalo riding with her.

"Well, this was a tough speech to write and I still feel like something is missing. It's not easy to 'share your wisdom' as I've been asked to do," responded Maria.

"Still, this must feel like a wonderful validation of you efforts in starting a new business after leaving Percipience Ltd.," continued Frida.

"Sure, but that isn't it. The car window just then reminded me of the feeling of the airplane window when I left Boston behind and headed for London all those years ago," mused Maria.

"Maria, you should not underestimate the power of that experience," Frida said as she took the back seat next to Maria.

"Yes, that was a hell of a chapter in my life, things really felt like they were spiraling out of control," Maria said, as she recentered herself on that memory.

Thinking back, Maria remembered those early years in Boston as a time of confidence, optimism, and happiness. Fresh out of school, Maria began working for a platform computing company called Nebulous, brimming with energy, enthusiasm, and high hopes. Soon after moving to Boston and in the glow of starting her new job, Maria had bought her first piece of real estate, a condominium on the Boston Harbor Wharf. While it was clearly a stretch on her salary, her parents co-signed the mortgage, and she was optimistic about her work prospects.

DOI: 10.4324/9781003491880-7

Maria's self-confidence was reinforced by her initial experiences with her clients in the Boston banking community. She quickly built great relationships through meetings in her clients' slick downtown offices and over memorable meals and drinks in all the right restaurants and bars.

"Maria, it's really impressive how quickly you've come to learn our business, it's almost like you're one of us," Jackie, the number two in the CTO organization of one of Maria's biggest clients said as she sipped a cocktail with Maria in a trendy Back Bay bar.

"I love working with you guys. I find your business so inspiring and dynamic. I'm learning a lot and it's exciting to be a partner in your success," Maria answered. "Cheers!"

Unfortunately, her positive start did not last very long. Despite the end of the "Great Recession," the economy never kicked in as expected, and Maria's infatuation with her clients prevented her from seeing the clouds on the horizon. During a client review meeting, her boss gave her some direct and challenging feedback, "Maria, you need to diversify your client base beyond the banking sector. It should not be hard for you to see the increasingly consistent news and events warning of a U.S. financial crisis."

"I just don't get it," Maria responded defensively. "My clients are projecting nothing but confidence, telling their customers not to worry and encouraging them to invest in brighter futures ahead. They are smart people whom I respect and trust (even as friends), so I why should I do anything differently?" Her boss responded by looking down and then straight into her eyes, "Maria, I hope I have been clear."

Despite the reinforcing challenges and warnings from her colleagues, Maria remained stubborn. By the time her clients were experiencing visible financial wobbles, it was much too late for anything but failure; Maria's sales plummeted, and with them, any chance of a promotion disappeared. More profoundly, Maria's future at Nebulous became palpably uncertain. She quickly found her mortgage payments challenging, even increasingly unrealistic. Each time she rode the elevator up to her apartment, she felt the burden of the condo mortgage dragging her down further and further. And then the next shoe dropped. Alejandro, whom she had been seeing seriously since meeting at the University of Maryland, had for some time been losing interest in their relationship. By the time she woke up to this, Alejandro was already seeing someone else, a fact which was eventually (and embarrassingly) pointed out to Maria by one of her closest friends.

As she reached out to her work colleagues for help and advice, she received little sympathy and support. They were facing their own challenges and career ramifications from the financial upheaval and had limited time and patience to hear about Maria's woes. In meetings with her boss, he focused the discussions on recovering banking client fees, avoiding any other topics. Maria's intense paranoia soon gave way to an acceptance of her dire situation.

As Maria faced up to the derailment of her first job, she realized that the personal, professional, and financial legs of her life seemed to be collapsing all at once. Leaving Nebulous was, by this point, either her asking to leave or being asked to do so. She was leaving, one way or another. Maria turned in her badge on her last day and squinted as she walked out into the sunshine of mid-day Boston, wondering how to grapple with the darkness ahead.

Maria returned to the present in her limo and shook her head. "Well, that period of my life sucked. Thanks for reminding me!" she said, turning her ire onto Frida Khalo, whom she imagined sitting beside her.

"Any time," smiled Frida. "Tell me, how did you dig out of that hole?"

Maria chuckled to herself and was back again in Boston.

The days that followed her exit from Nebulous were dark and sad. Maria hunkered down at her condo, and when she did venture out, she felt in many ways self-conscious and embarrassed. She had trouble sleeping and her appetite faded. Most terrifying to Maria was her mental state. She continuously felt like she was moving downward, driven by relentless, almost obsessive thoughts of her failures. I quit my first job, who will hire me? How will I pay my mortgage and living expenses? What happens when my health insurance ends? *She felt like she was tumbling into darkness. It was like nothing she had ever experienced.*

At first, sharing her woes with her friends and family only made Maria feel depressed and victimized. They responded with clichéd advice on how she could use this time to recover and agreed with her that it was less her fault than it was the fault of Nebulous. Maria did her best to appreciate their offers of genuine personal support. Unfortunately, their help felt like pity to her, convincing Maria that she was in profound trouble.

After a week or so, Maria met a friend for a bag lunch in Boston Common. "Maria, what actually happened at Nebulous?" her friend asked. Maria realized it was the first time that anyone had really asked that question. She had been turning the events over and over in her mind but now she needed to tell the story.

"Well, I want to say it was complicated and unavoidable but that wouldn't really be true," Maria said. Then she spent the next 20 minutes telling the story of the past 6 months. At times, she was the hero, at other times, the victim, and, at still others, she was the driver who drove the car off a cliff. She talked about her financial challenges, her work challenges, and even about her relationship issues. Sharing and reflecting on what happened was awkward and hard. And this was not the only time she would tell the story. Over the days that followed, Maria took the opportunity to tell the story again and again to friends and family and she began to see and understand some new perspectives on what had happened. She saw herself less as a victim and more as an active participant in the journey that had led to her losing her job. She saw the moments when the tide of events had swept her away, and how she had missed the chances to guide her future.

Not long after, Maria found herself in a Starbucks with a latte and a notebook. On a blank page she wrote the question: "Who am I and who do I want to be?" She began taking stock of her experiences in a way she had never done before. Six months later, she was off to London. Twenty years after that, she was smiling at an empty seat in the back of a limo, imagining an approving nod from Frida Kahlo.

Duh – We Learn from Experience

People learn from experience. Leaders, being people, also learn from experience. Perhaps a more obvious statement has never been written; and countless theorists and authors have been making this point forever. Since the late 1980s beginning with research by Michael Lombardo and Morgan McCall[1] at the Center for Creative Leadership, the practice of leadership development has been driven by the so-called "Lessons of Experience" model. A plethora of models, systems, and processes emerged from this, probably the most well-known being the concept of "70/20/10." This is a formula for strategically apportioning development efforts, along the lines of what has the most impact: 70% of development through experiences on the job; 20% via relationships (mentoring and advice); and 10% via formal learning.

The logic of formulas like these is that we can learn from all types of experiences, both positive and negative. Moreover, the more impactful the experience, the deeper the learning. And yet simply looking around at the people in our lives – and at ourselves – shows us that while learning from experience is possible, it is far from guaranteed. This is especially evident when we go through deeply seminal experiences that only begin to reveal themselves as times of great potential learning in hindsight. To quote the Danish philosopher Soren Kierkegaard, "Life is lived forwards but understood backwards."

In the story that opened this chapter, Maria descends into a dark period, experiencing professional failure partly of her own making, a relationship falling apart, and personal financial missteps that added pressure across all areas of her life. And while she ultimately grew as a result, any of us who have walked down a similar dark street in their own life know that growth is in no way a predictable outcome. Extremely positive events can offer moments of significant learning opportunities as well. For example, when you absolutely crush an almost impossible challenge in work or your personal life and, for a moment, you reach the top of the mountain, looking down at the world you've just conquered, that is certainly a learning experience. But all too often, we fail to walk away with new wisdom. The question then is, how can you learn from this moment and find the ability to turn your approach into repeated success rather than just moving on or resting on your laurels? That is our task in this chapter: to understand the *how* of learning from experience in order to increase the likelihood that, as you step through the crucible experiences of your life, you view them as opportunities for growth.

As with every other aspect of leadership, your personal development is an opportunity to demonstrate agency: to step forward with purposeful intent and actively seek to draw and apply lessons from your experiences. The essence of learning from experience is to seize an experience and actively guide yourself through it to grow, rather than simply appearing as a character passively living through an experience driven by others.

It is our view that the guidance available to help us develop leadership capacity is limited to encouraging us to curate experiences of maximum impact, to build checklists of the types of experiences we should have and then to seek them out. However, "how" you can learn from living through a meaningful experience is rarely discussed. We are not given actionable steps. And that is why we have created an Agency Model for leadership development – which is focused on *how* to learn from experience and, crucially *doing something as a result of this learning: translating growth to action*. We see this as an important evolution of the existing state of thinking around learning through experience.

The "how" of experiential learning begins with agency. Learning from experience requires two key steps: one, making a *conscious choice* to extract growth, learning, and even wisdom from the experiences of your life rather than passively moving through them; and two, having a clear ambition regarding the direction of your growth. Purposeful intent and ambition, the foundations of personal agency, become the engine driving the "how" of learning from development.

Before we share our model, we must look at two critical concepts that are central to leadership development: *simultaneity* and *growth through adversity*. Understanding these concepts is a prerequisite for learning *how* to develop through experience.

Simultaneity

The writer/poet Clint Smith defines *simultaneity* as the "ability to hold two different beliefs concurrently. How joy sits along sorrow. How wonder sits along despair. How we carry it all at once." In understanding this concept, it is useful to consider his poem "All at Once" which explains it eloquently:

> The redwoods are on fire in California. A flood submerges a neighborhood that sat quiet at the coast for three centuries. A child takes their first steps and tumbles into a father's arms. Two people in New Orleans fall in love under an oak tree whose branches bend like sorrow. A forest of seeds are planted in new soil. A glacier melts into the ocean and the sea climbs closer to the land. A man comes home from war and holds his son for the first time. A man is killed by a drone that thinks his jug of water is a bomb. Your best friend relapses and isn't picking up the phone. Your son's teacher calls to say he stood up for another boy in class. A country below the equator ends a twenty-year civil war. A soldier across the Atlantic fires the shot that begins another. The scientists find a vaccine that will save millions of people's lives. Your mother's cancer has returned and doctors say there is nothing else they can do. There is a funeral procession in the morning and a wedding in the afternoon. The river that gives us water to drink is the same one that might wash us away.

> Clint Smith, "All at Once," *Above Ground* – 2023[2]

Successfully learning from everyday experience, and from deeper crucible experiences, requires an understanding of simultaneity. Simultaneity is about being able to see the depths and complex intertwining of your challenges as clearly as you can, in order to frame the options and opportunities that lie ahead. The idea of simultaneity – holding paradoxical views simultaneously in your mind – remains challenging in any circumstance, especially so in the service of your own personal growth because the stakes touch you so directly.

Simultaneity may sound like it flies in the face of the concept of cognitive dissonance; the notion that it is not possible to hold conflicting views simultaneously. According to Festinger's[3] idea of cognitive dissonance, when we are confronted with two paradoxical thoughts, we have only three options: we must deny one, change one, or add a third thought to make it acceptable to hold the competing ideas. Simultaneity, however, offers a fourth option which is about not making that choice, but rather accepting and reconciling yourself to the inherent paradox, in order to move forward and grow. Maria's triumph in the story that starts this chapter was realizing that she could learn from failure, have hope during pain, and find a way to move forward. We can almost hear her think, "I have just failed utterly and I am feeling devastated by the failure, but I can learn and grow from this pain."

Achieving simultaneity requires approaching paradox with an important attitude: hope through confidence. In our collective experience of coaching hundreds of executives around the world, those who are able to grow through deeply personally impactful experiences are able to build some version of hope through a belief that "I can take this and learn from it." They are able to express confidence and hope, stepping up to the biggest "balcony" of them all and rising above the tensions or apparent limitations of the situation. They are able to experience and draw upon what Rebecca Solnit eloquently describes as the "spaciousness of uncertainty."[4] They are immersed in the tide as well as guiding it!

To successfully pass through the seminal moments in your life and to grow, you must begin with this mindset of simultaneity. It is exemplified by a willingness to continually step forward into experience and to hold the totality of the apparent chaos of simultaneity in your mind. It is nurtured by finding hope through confidence in your ability for sensemaking and for growth. The realization of this perspective ultimately becomes a resource for resilience, as leaders evolve from hubris to humility rooted in a crucial admission: "The world is unpredictable, dynamic and flawed – and so are we. It's an approach that recognizes that the strength of knowledge – and of our own minds – derives from its very mutability. It's a realm of second chances."[5]

Growth through Adversity (and Success) – the Bounce

Adversity has been recognized as one of the most powerful development catalysts, based on the insight that we learn best in the face of obstacles. The idea of growth through adversity as a leadership-development opportunity took root some 40 years ago as researchers who interviewed top leaders found a common theme. These leaders consistently perceived their most serious challenges – failure, bad bosses, demotions, missed promotions, shake-ups, politics, or terminations – as their most impactful development moments. As Warren Bennis explained in the classic book, *Becoming a Leader:*[6]

> In 1817, poet John Keats wrote in a letter to his brothers that the basis for real achievement was "negative capability … when a man is capable of being in uncertainties, mysteries, doubts, without any irritable reaching after the fact and reason." There's probably no better definition of a contemporary leader than that.

When facing moments of significant adversity, you have two choices. You can wallow in the depths of the deep darkness that adversity can bring: a horrific funk of victimization and/or self-recrimination leading to an endless cycle of rumination causing you to stagnate.[7] Or, you can rise up and "bounce" to a new level of productive behavior. This is the so-called *post-traumatic growth*. As Bob Thomas describes in his ground-breaking book, *The Crucibles of Leadership*[8] the "ability to find meaning and strength in adversity" is "what distinguishes leaders from non-leaders."

In the prior chapter we described the core elements of successfully navigating a "bounce"[9] from a challenge (and avoiding the alternative!) and we want to repeat them here. Keep in mind that these same factors are also essential when you are seeking to grow from a success.

- Resetting your worldview – Your worldview or "assumptive schema" is your set of fundamental assumptions about how the world works. Although not easy, no development can take place unless you learn to examine the beliefs and assumptions that underpin how you think and respond to the world. Your task is to challenge your assumptive schema when reality does not match expectations and face up to the new truths that may be staring at you in the face.

- <u>Seeking support</u> – Successfully resetting your frame of mind and managing negative thoughts and emotions is difficult and perhaps better done with the support of others. However, emotional regulation is also a personal task; it involves being mindful of your emotions, observing them, and focusing on best-case possibilities. It requires shifting from what you cannot do to what you can do. Seeking feedback and tuning in to observe yourself from the outside-in can raise your awareness of how you come across to others.
- <u>Telling your story</u> – Disclosing what is and what has happened to you and talking about its effects and what you are struggling with are critical to growth. According to Richard Tedeschi,[10] this articulation is "what helps us make sense of the trauma and turn debilitating thoughts into more productive reflections." This is evident in Maria's story and how she eventually begins to emerge from her crucible through revisiting and shaping the narrative of her experience in conversations with family and friends.

THE *HOW* OF LEARNING FROM EXPERIENCE

Having covered these two concepts of simultaneity and bounce, we can now share what we call our "Agency Model" for leadership development (Figure 7.1).

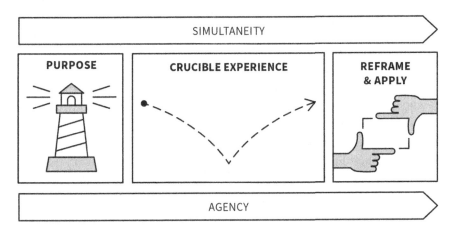

FIGURE 7.1
The Growth Bounce

The model is built from five components that comprise any human undertaking: a starting point, a mindset, a foundation, a set of behaviors, and an application of these behaviors to a problem.

Starting point	=	**Purpose**
Mindset	=	**Simultaneity**
Behaviors	=	**Growth Bounce**
Application	=	**Reframe and Apply**
Foundation	=	**Agency**

Let's take a look at how these concepts come together in an integrated "Agency" model, an approach to the "how" of bridging the distance from experience to meaningful wisdom.

Your Starting Point: Purpose

The model begins with anchoring your development efforts in your *Purpose*. Purpose is the foundation which allows you to move forward through meaningful experiences with confidence and helps you build a vision for the impact you wish to create. As we navigate the tide around us – the ever-changing stream of systems, technology, society, consumers, competitors, and human energy – your purpose helps to steady and center you. It prevents you from getting swept away by the tide. And, if crucible experiences are the rapids within the tide, purpose allows you to approach them with confidence.

As we've explained before, purpose is central to our model that produces Honest Engagement. Purpose supports the sustainable energy that drives our ability to successfully Guide the Tide. Without this mature, deep sense of who you are, what you want to become, and the role you want to express in the world, your ability to learn, grow, and thrive will be severely handicapped. Given the importance of your purpose in both building the capability for Honest Engagement and anchoring you to learn from experience, let's take a moment to review how you can discover your sense of purpose.

Defining a sense of purpose can be challenging, not least because it can shift and change over the course of our lives. And yet, the foundational

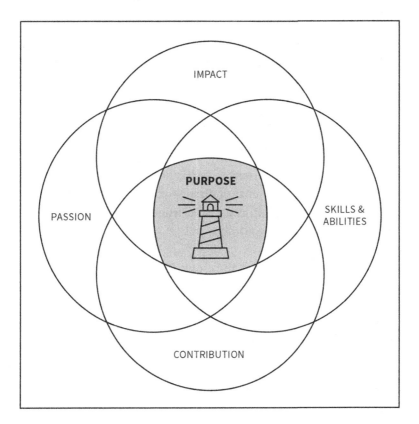

FIGURE 7.2
Understanding Purpose

elements of purpose remain constant: impact, contribution, passion, skills, and abilities.[11] We took an in-depth look at finding your sense of purpose in Chapter 3 (Figure 7.2). As the anchor of your development, purpose is so critical: we will repeat here the essential elements of uncovering your purpose.

Asking these four questions is the key to discovering your purpose:

1. What am I most passionate about?
2. What impact do I want to help create?
3. What is the contribution I can make to create that impact?
4. What skills and abilities can I bring to the table to make this contribution?

These four considerations help center your purpose. Having a sense of purpose shifts the dynamic of living through crucible experiences from asking: "What does this crucible say about what the world/life is all about?" to seeking out the answer to "How does this experience help me understand what I am and should be all about?"

Your Critical Mindset: Simultaneity

The "messiness" of your experiences, particularly adverse ones, will inevitably call upon you to make sense of dissonant, often paradoxical realities. As described above, approaching an experience with an attitude of simultaneity requires you to do two things:

1. Choose to accept rather than resolve the paradox – this experience can be both painful and beneficial at the same time; it can be both a triumph and an opportunity to see gaps in your abilities.
2. Having hope for your ability to turn the experience into growth based on a sense of personal confidence.

Growth through Adversity (and Success) – the Bounce to Build New Behaviors

> The greatest glory in living lies not in never falling but in rising every time we fall.
>
> **Nelson Mandela**

While learning from success has its own challenges (avoiding hubris, for example), much of the most referenced leadership research has focused on learning from adversity. Whether positive or negative, deeply meaningful and impactful experiences give you the opportunity (but not a guarantee) to grow. The first step in learning from an experience is to step up to the balcony and see yourself in action, while you are still in action. This is the essence of how exceptional leaders approach growing from the high-impact moments in their lives. Create space for yourself to assess your actions, to "see" yourself and very honestly assess what you are doing that is productive and what is non-productive.

Once you can see yourself in action, it is time to put to use what we described in our "prerequisites" above as the way to process adversity and success:

1. Be willing to adjust your worldview – surface, examine, and adjust your working assumptions.
2. Seek support from others to make sense of the experience by drawing on others' reflections and feedback; use others as sounding boards and to vent frustrations.
3. Frame the experience into a compelling story that creates meaning and clarifies what lessons you are drawing from the experience.

Agency as a Foundation

The final component, most critically, is to retain your sense of agency. This is easier said than done. When living through a difficult, impactful, stressful experience, it can be easy to see yourself as a victim of circumstances in which your behavior is shaped by forces you cannot control. In fact, it can be rewarding to see yourself as a victim, gaining sympathy, support, and even the emotional uplift of shared outrage with those around you.[12] This is a trap that stifles growth. Remember that you cannot control the tide, but you are in control of your actions. Take accountability for your behavior, assess it, and, most importantly, make the choice to learn from it.

Application: Reframe and Apply

Surviving a crucible moment and drawing meaning, even learning, from it is not enough, as Maria Miller's career should attest. True growth occurs when you can take the insights you've gained from one seminal moment and discover ways to apply them across many varied situations.[13] This is the need to reframe your approach and apply this reframing to a broad range of new situations. This is the manifestation of your leadership growth. As resources to your own work in reframing and applying wisdom, we share these concepts from Tedeschi:[14]

- <u>Narrative development</u> – Building on the concept of "Telling your story," narrative development means crafting the story about what happens beyond the crucible experience: what happens next. This will allow you to accept what has happened and help you to imagine and move forward toward a positive future.
- <u>Service</u> – Tedeschi describes this as finding "work that benefits others", and helping people close to you or your broader community. This is not limited to being of service, it also encompasses expressing gratitude and/or showing empathy to others. These efforts can help energize you and further help you find meaning. This concept of service is fundamental, and it differentiates the most successful leaders with whom we have worked.

IN SUMMARY

The ultimate lesson of experience must be more than new wisdom or growth; you must translate your newly acquired wisdom into action. New learning, capabilities, and wisdom are akin to the idea of potential energy in physics in that it is real, it is important, but it is latent. Only when potential energy is translated into kinetic energy – motion, impact, action – does it become meaningful. The real opportunity is to move forward, stepping into and guiding the tide around you in a more effective manner with deeper self-knowledge, a clearer view of Addressing Reality, and with greater Adaptive Impact. It is a dynamic that the best leaders we've worked with have mastered and it is our hope this you learn to see this opportunity in a way that inspires you to reach for the same level of achievement.

In this chapter we have revisited the historical, accepted truths of leadership development grounded in the lessons of experience approach. The fundamental truth that this research provides is that we do learn from experience. We have tried to expand this foundation by spending some time introducing and detailing our "Agency Model" for leadership development as a resource to explain how to learn from experience. It should be obvious that the Agency Model for development is based on many of the concepts of leadership we have discussed more broadly as necessary to guiding the tide. Development – your development – is just as essential to successfully leading with agency as is Honest Engagement, Addressing Reality, and Adaptive Impact. And it takes the same effort – stepping intentionally into the tide and guiding it to an outcome that is beneficial and productive for you and for those around you.

As the limo pulled up at the hotel hosting the W3 Summit where she was about to give her address, Maria began to reframe her remarks. She intended to focus less on the events of her life, and more on the impact these events had on her, how she had learned from both the good and bad experiences, the highs and lows across her career. She would share her reflections on how she made sense of the ambiguities and dualities. She would encourage the audience to appreciate their purpose, to listen and communicate, to convey confidence while maintaining humility, and to remain closely focused but also to step onto the balcony. She was excited to discuss how she had defined her story and how she continued to step into her world.

NOTES

1 Morgan W. McCall, Michael M. Lombardo, and Ann M. Morrison, *The Lessons of Experience: How Successful Executives Develop on the Job* (Lexington, Mass: Lexington Books, 1988).

2 Clint Smith, *Above Ground: Poems*, First edition (New York: Little, Brown and Company, 2023).

3 Leon Festinger, *A Theory of Cognitive Dissonance*, Re-issued by Stanford Univ. Press in 1962, renewed 1985 by author [Nachdr.] (Stanford, Calif: Stanford Univ. Press, 2001).

4 Rebecca Solnit, *Hope in the Dark: Untold Histories, Wild Possibilities*, Third edition with a new foreword and afterword (Chicago, Illinois: Haymarket Books, 2016).

5 Maggie Jackson, "How to Thrive in an Uncertain World," *The New York Times* (January 14, 2024), New York edition, sec. SR.

6 Bennis, *On Becoming a Leader*.

7 Manfred F.R. Kets de Vries, "The Art of Forgiveness: Differentiating Transformational Leaders," Faculty and Research Working Paper, 2013, https://sites.insead.edu/facultyresearch/research/doc.cfm?did=52275.

8 Robert J. Thomas, *Crucibles of Leadership: How to Learn from Experience to Become a Great Leader* (Boston, Mass: Harvard Business Press, 2008).

9 Tedeschi and Calhoun, ""Posttraumatic Growth."

10 Richard G. Tedeschi, "Growth After Trauma," *Harvard Business Review*, July 2020, https://hbr.org/2020/07/growth-after-trauma.

11 Palsule and Chavez, *Rehumanizing Leadership*.
12 Manfred F.R. Kets de Vries, *Mindful Leadership Coaching: Journeys into the Interior*, INSEAD Business Press Series (Basingstoke: Palgrave Macmillan, 2014).
13 Guglielmo and Palsule, *The Social Leader*.
14 Tedeschi, "Growth After Trauma."

Epilogue

STEPPING FORWARD

We began writing just at the start of the pandemic and here we are, a few years later. As we alluded to in the Introduction, we set out to write this book for *you*: for those of you engaged in leading organizations and people, for the leadership practitioners and thinkers, for those tasked with designing leadership development initiatives, and for all those curious about what it means to lead in the complex 21st-century context.

From the very beginning of this project, our purpose has been about making a compelling case for leadership agency. Our initial conversation in that Cambridge, Massachusetts bar confirmed our unified frustration and a shared fear about our observations and experiences of leadership. We were noticing a decreasing leadership agency exemplified by a growing hesitancy, reticence, and even resignation in leaders in the face of the dynamic and daunting challenges of today's world. We were struck by just how just dire the impact of this trend can be, especially considering that at this time in our history, leadership agency could not be more critical.

So the goal of this book is not to reframe, redefine, or even review the well-worn discussions around reacting to the challenges of complexity. Instead, our aim is to help leaders proactively guide complexity. It is that difference that we believe will make *the* difference. We set out to define a new way into complexity: leaders must rise above the numbing and learn to embrace a new way of leading, developing resilience, and building hope. You can only do this through a deeper understanding of your purpose and values, the reality that surrounds you, and of the impact you need to create. You have only two choices: to succumb to unfamiliar complexity by labeling it VUCA or some other clever acronym and thus placing it outside of your ability to impact, or you can rise up and bounce to a higher level of understanding and ability and seek to guide the tide of complexity, even if it cannot be controlled or completely predicted. This is a deeply personal decision and a challenging call to action.

DOI: 10.4324/9781003491880-8

A QUICK REFLECTION

We made Maria and her muse, Frida Kahlo, our companions throughout the book as we explored the 21st-century tide and what it means to step into it and guide it. We wrote about the critical practices necessary to step into and guide the tide through our stories about Maria. We saw her grapple with challenging experiences, confront deeply held assumptions and worldviews, and emerge from these experiences with a renewed sense of purpose and clarity. Maria is every one of us: ambitious, well-meaning, talented, sincere, hard-working, and subject to the tide with all its ebbs and flows. We hope that you had insights into yourself through Maria, as she learned to step into the tide and guide it.

What we also hope you saw in Maria, and what we hope you see in yourself, is that it is not an easy task to face adversity, to bounce up and grow in the face of life's most challenging moments. However, true leaders embrace this reality with vision and conviction, guiding themselves and others toward positive change and a brighter future. We saw the need for this new set of approaches to step into and guide a far more complex tide. We distilled these approaches into the form of three practices that became the core of this book: Honest Engagement, Addressing Reality, and Adaptive Impact (Figure 8.1).

You engage honestly when you deal with situations and others from a place of openness, candor, and a willingness to be vulnerable. It goes beyond rational decision-making and making informed choices. Instead, it centers on aligning your actions with your core values and purpose, while simultaneously considering the broader impact you have on the people and organizations you lead. Honest Engagement involves bringing together your autobiographical perspective (What must I do?) and your biographical perspective (What am I being called upon to do?). When you practice Honest Engagement, you necessarily bring together a deep awareness of yourself, a keen sense of empathy, and the ability to authentically communicate and connect with others. Honest Engagement is the cornerstone of guiding the tide, leading with purpose, and making a positive impact on the world.

Addressing Reality is about actively seeking information, interpreting it objectively by managing your biases and assumption, and enrolling others in the work of understanding the tide that is sweeping past you, while

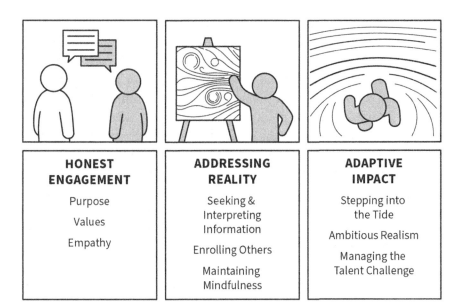

HONEST ENGAGEMENT	ADDRESSING REALITY	ADAPTIVE IMPACT
Purpose Values Empathy	Seeking & Interpreting Information Enrolling Others Maintaining Mindfulness	Stepping into the Tide Ambitious Realism Managing the Talent Challenge

FIGURE 8.1
Guiding the Tide Practices

maintaining a state of mindfulness to stay focused on what is crucial, and understanding the broader context. It is critical that you perceive the world as it truly is, rather than how you might wish it to be, separating data from desire and fact from fiction. As you can imagine, this is easier said than done as the human brain has a proclivity toward projecting its unconscious desires and biases and fabricating the projected image as reality. It is far easier to be deluded than to be clear sighted!

When you practice Adaptive Impact, you must necessarily step into the tide and challenge prevailing assumptions. In the process, you will create meaningful disruptions. You will need to embody what we call Ambitious Realism, by staying close to, and blending together, the stories of what was, what is, and what could be. That is how you build resources for staying relevant, deliver value efficiently, and bring out the best in your people by fostering a culture of constant curiosity and skill development. Practicing Adaptive Impact is recognizing that you must work within the complex, ever-changing tide of systems, technology, society, consumers, and competitors, which is driven by human energy. It needs you to stay humble so that you can acknowledge that the story you create exists within the tide you must shape.

Staying humble sounds easy but it is more than self-importance that gets in its way. It can also be the autopilot of knowledge and experience. After all, when you have been in a leadership role for decades and have been successful, it is easy and natural to slip unconsciously into the "knowing" mode. We came up with the term "Humble Safari" as a prompt to nudge you into practicing "not knowing." Remember, it is so easy to think you know. This is especially true when you are being validated by the people around you, who either do not want to challenge you, or who think the same way you do. The Humble Safari is a process that helps you step out of your comfortable world and engage in conversations and inquiry.

Finally, we positioned leadership as delivering results-beyond-results. Yes, the targeted goals are critical but so are the ones that are often difficult to target. "*...everything that counts cannot necessarily be counted,*" as Einstein once said. Among those difficult-to-count goals are followership, sustainability, and Humanocity in the workplace. Annual engagement reviews and corporate social responsibility (CSR) measures are useful tools, but they do not serve as guides to leadership. Results-beyond-results is an everyday goal and not some big event or an initiative. You are creating your leadership legacy now, not in some distant future. Remember, it is the moments you live now that will become the life you will look back on!

We wanted to provoke a conversation around the idea that leaders can and should see themselves as the authors of the story that is unfolding around them, rather than being characters merely driven along by the plot. "Guiding the tide" was a way of describing what we have been recognizing as the skillful juxtaposition of two actions: move forward proactively and do it from a place of great humility!

To effectively guide the tide, you must achieve a unique perspective: maintaining the capacity for reflection while in action. This skill has often been described as "*getting off the dance floor and going to the balcony.*" However, obtaining and retaining this perspective can be challenging when you are the protagonist in your own development story. Watch out for complacency and hubris! That is why we wrote about creating a cycle of renewal, marked by three core steps: Step Back, Let Go, and Step Forward.

"Step Back" involves periodically moving to the balcony, so that you can observe yourself and your impact and assess your progress in achieving goals like enhancing followership, sustainability, and Humanocity in the workplace. "Let Go" entails transitioning from a state of success and comfort to something new, and to becoming comfortable with discomfort. "Step Forward" is about setting new goals and finding opportunities that align with your values, capabilities, and desired impact. We encouraged you to actively create your own crucibles while avoiding inertia or passively waiting for opportunities to arise.

In essence, the paradox of guiding the tide challenges you to continuously evolve by balancing introspection with action and thereby shaping your own leadership story. In most leadership development models, the trajectory of development has been rooted in guided experiences, often driven by personal ambition, the desire for recognition, and a focus on climbing the hierarchical ladder. While these elements remain important, learning to guide the tide as a 21st-century leader requires a different set of dynamics and a deep shift in mindset and capabilities. You must focus on four key components: purpose, simultaneity, growth, and reframing and applying your insights across various situations.

A LOOK FORWARD

It does feel like we have been on a voyage with you over the last few years. The world has witnessed two major conflicts that are ongoing, with no signs of resolution any time soon. Whatever happens, the fallout is going to be significant for decades to come. It seems evident that the cracks of polarization across the globe are going to become deeper and even more present in our everyday lives, setting the stage for deglobalization. Climate change continues to be an extremely serious concern – not as an isolated problem but as a trigger for a whole host of issues including food, water, and large-scale human migration.

Then there is the juggernaut of digital technology and generative AI that is moving ahead at a frenetic pace. Artificial Intelligence brings both the promise of a new world of automation and smart living along with the fears of unregulated technology going rogue. Generative AI is no longer a tool for crawling the Internet and processing information, but it is already exhibiting thinking and learning patterns. The greatest danger from AI lies in its mimicking human speech and emotions, thereby creating a sense of false intimacy and influencing our judgment. In January 2024, 350 AI industry leaders, including Sam Altman, who is CEO of the ChatGPT creator OpenAI, signed a statement calling for global priority to be placed on mitigating the risk of "extinction" from AI.

Yes, these are complex global problems on a scale likely a few steps removed from your immediate leadership issues. But they remain as real as the issues you face directly, and like it or not, they will impact the markets you serve, the people you lead, and the workplaces you manage. The world will only get more complex and so will the world of your organizations and businesses. The tide is here, and you can and must step into it; it is no longer possible to lead from the shore. You might have been able to do that in a relatively less complex world defined by the Industrial Age and for much of the previous century, but no longer.

The 20th century trained us for linearity, not simultaneity; for control, not adaptability; and for predictability, not emergence. We are not exaggerating when we say that we are faced with a crisis of meaning. The old, familiar world order is crumbling before our eyes, and a profoundly unknown one is starting to take its place. Yes, humanity has been through such epochs before, and this is certainly not the first time we are being faced with such a crisis. But it will require a call to leadership on the part of all of us. Learning to use Agency to guide the tide is vital and inescapable unless we wish to simply give in to submission.

The initial discussions that led to this book included not only our observations on the decline of agency in leaders but also consideration of our own (and our profession's) roles in bringing this about. We reflected on our work with leaders to create world-class leadership development and growth over the past four decades: the words we have used in our writing, coaching, and teaching, and the premises, models, and concepts on which our teachings have been based. To what extent had we addressed – or collaborated with – this decline of leadership agency? Given our long careers in this profession, we took a hard look at our own roles in the decline of agency.

Our insights were both helpful and humbling. We are confident and proud of how our work has impacted leaders' ability to build important and meaningful perspectives on core themes such as the "lessons" of experience, the bedrock resources of values and purpose, the maturing power of self-awareness and authenticity, the profound opportunities of a systems perspective, and a much deeper understanding and appreciation of complexity. So many of the leaders we've worked with have gone forward to shape organizational success and constructively inspire followers.

Yet we are also facing up to the realization that this same work may also have played a role, even indirectly, with the decline of agency and promotion of a stance of leadership inertia. And so we began to examine our work with an acceptance that we would need to challenge our own long-held, accepted premises and confidence in our thinking, with the goal of exposing it to the rigor of questions around "so what?" and "how to step forward, even into complexity."

What we are asking from you is that you do the same thing. Strive to develop yourself in a way that is based on deep and highly personal reflection, a structured adventure into what makes you a productive leader. The Maria stories throughout the book are based on our experiences with executives around the world; they are intended as resources to help you recognize and understand what is being asked of leaders now and in the future. We fervently hope that you remain curious, that you keep growing, and keep stepping forward into the complexity in order to make a greater positive impact in the world. We hope you see yourself and your opportunities in Maria's story.

Further, we hope this book has not just provoked you to think differently, but that it has given you a mindset and a set of tools to work with to further your leadership journey. We offer you the encouragement to strive forward with hope.

> Hope is not optimism, which expects things to turn out well, but something rooted in the conviction that there is good worth working for.
>
> - Seamus Heaney

A FINAL WORD

As we said at the opening, leadership is a choice you make, not an entitlement or a reward. You can find the personal agency to choose to step into the tide and guide it from within. Ultimately, leadership is about two things: who you are and how you show up. Who you are is your biggest and arguably your only real resource. How you show up determines the impact you have on the world.

Throughout this book, we have used Frida Kahlo as a literary device to help express and reflect the inner dialogue of our heroine, Maria Miller, along her journey to Leadership Agency. It was never our intention to suggest that Kahlo was the inspiration for these thoughts on leadership, merely that she served as our "Greek Chorus" and a muse in whom Maria felt comfortable confiding and questioning; a soundboard Maria could count on. Just as Dante had Virgil, Frodo had Sam, and Superman had Lois Lane, Maria had Frida. And so, having relied on the imagined voice of the great Frida Kahlo throughout this book, we feel it is only fitting to give her the last word:

> They thought I was a surrealist, but I wasn't. I never painted dreams. I painted my own reality.
>
> Frida Kahlo

Over to you.

Bibliography

Bandura, A. (1962). Social learning through imitation. In M. R. Jones (Ed.), *Nebraska Symposium on Motivation* (pp. 211–274). University of Nebraska Press.

Bennis, W. G. (2009). *On Becoming a Leader* (20th anniversary ed.) Basic Books.

Bethune, S., & Brownawell, A. (2010). *Americans Report Willpower and Stress as Key Obstacles to Meeting Health-Related Resolutions* [Press Release]. American Psychological Association. https://www.apa.org/news/press/releases/2010/03/lifestyle-changes

Bloom, P. (2016). *Against Empathy: The Case for Rational Compassion* (First ed.) Ecco, an imprint of HarperCollins Publishers.

Bowling, N. A., & Schumm, J. A. (2021). The COVID-19 pandemic: A source of posttraumatic growth? *Industrial and Organizational Psychology, 14*(1–2), 184–188. https://doi.org/10.1017/iop.2021.31

Boyatzis, R. E., Goleman, D., Dhar, U., & Osiri, J. K. (2021). Thrive and survive: Assessing personal sustainability. *Consulting Psychology Journal: Practice and Research, 73*(1), 27–50. https://doi.org/10.1037/cpb0000193

Campbell, J. (2008). *The Hero with a Thousand Faces* (Third ed.) New World Library.

Campbell, J., & Walter, R. (2017). *A Joseph Campbell Companion: Reflections on the Art of Living*. Joseph Campbell Foundation.

Clarke, A. C. (1985). *Profiles of the Future: An Inquiry into the Limits of the Possible* (Third rev. ed.) Grand Central Publishing.

Coffey, C. (2020). *Time to care: Unpaid and underpaid care work and the global inequality crisis*. Oxfam International.

Colvin, G. (2016). *Humans are Underrated: What High Achievers Know that Brilliant Machines Never Will* (Paperback ed.). Portfolio Penguin.

Deci, E. L., & Ryan, R. M. (2000). The "what" and "why" of goal pursuits: Human needs and the self-determination of behavior. *Psychological Inquiry, 11*(4), 227–268. https://doi.org/10.1207/S15327965PLI1104_01

Festinger, L. (2001). *A Theory of Cognitive Dissonance* (Re-issued by Stanford Univ. Press in 1962, renewed 1985 by author [Nachdr.]). Stanford University Press.

Friedman, T. L. (2022, January 5). How to stop Trump and prevent another Jan. 6. *The New York Times, 18*.

Fromm, E. (2006). *The Art of Loving* (50th anniversary Modern classics ed.) Harper Perennial.

Frost, R. (1915, August). The road not taken and other poems. *The Atlantic Monthly*. https://www.theatlantic.com/magazine/archive/1915/08/a-group-of-poems/306620/

Gentile, M. C. (2012). *Giving Voice to Values: How to Speak Your Mind When You Know What's Right*. Yale University Press.

Guglielmo, F., & Palsule, S. (2014). *The Social Leader: Redefining Leadership for the Complex Social Age*. Bibliomotion.

Hall, R. (2020, March 11). Analyst who predicted 2008 global financial crash warns another one is on the way – And not just because of coronavirus. *The Independent UK*. https://www.independent.co.uk/news/world/americas/financial-crisis-2008-coronavirus-donald-trump-economy-stocks-a9392881.html

Harari, Y. N. (2015). *Sapiens: A Brief History of Humankind* (First U.S. ed.). Harper.

Heifetz, R. A., Grashow, A., & Linsky, M. (2009). *The Practice of Adaptive Leadership: Tools and Tactics for Changing Your Organization and the World*. Harvard Business Press.

Heifetz, R. A., & Linsky, M. (2002, June). A survival guide for leaders. *Harvard Business Review*. https://hbr.org/2002/06/a-survival-guide-for-leaders

Hogan, R., Kaiser, R. B., Sherman, R. A., & Harms, P. D. (2021). Twenty years on the dark side: Six lessons about bad leadership. *Consulting Psychology Journal: Practice and Research, 73*(3), 199–213. https://doi.org/10.1037/cpb0000205

Horney, K. (1937). *The Collected Works of Karen Horney* (Vol. 1). W. W. Norton Inc.

Houston, J. (n.d.). *Being a Social Artist* [Audio Recording]. https://www.awakin.org/v2/read/view.php?op=audio&tid=424

Ibarra, H. (2015). *Act Like a Leader, Think Like a Leader*. Harvard Business Review Press.

Ibarra, H., Rattan, A., & Johnston, A. (2008). *Satya Nadella at Microsoft: Instilling a Growth Mindset* [Case Study]. London Business School. https://hbsp.harvard.edu/product/LBS128-PDF-ENG

IPCC. (2022). *Global Warming of 1.5°C: IPCC Special Report on Impacts of Global Warming of 1.5 C above Pre-industrial Levels in Context of Strengthening Response to Climate Change, Sustainable Development, and Efforts to Eradicate Poverty* (1st ed.) Cambridge University Press. https://doi.org/10.1017/9781009157940

Jackson, M. (2024, January 14). How to thrive in an uncertain world. *The New York Times*, 10.

Janoff-Bulman, R. (1989). Assumptive worlds and the stress of traumatic events: Applications of the schema construct. *Social Cognition, 7*(2), 113–136. https://doi.org/10.1521/soco.1989.7.2.113

Johansen, B. (2017). *The New Leadership Literacies: Thriving in a Future of Extreme Disruption and Distributed Everything* (First ed.) BK, Berrett-Koehler Publishers, Inc.

Kahneman, D., Rosenfield, A. M., Gandhi, L., & Blaser, T. (2016, October). Noise: How to overcome the high, hidden cost of inconsistent decision making. *Harvard Business Review, 94*(10), 38–46.

Kanter, R. M. (2011, November). How great companies think differently. *Harvard Business Review*. https://hbr.org/2011/11/how-great-companies-think-differently

Kegan, R. (1997). *In Over Our Heads: The Mental Demands of Modern Life* (4th print). Harvard University Press.

Kets de Vries, M. F. R. (2013). *The Art of Forgiveness: Differentiating Transformational Leaders*. INSEAD Faculty and Research Working Paper. https://sites.insead.edu/facultyresearch/research/doc.cfm?did=52275

Kets de Vries, M. F. R. (2014). *Mindful Leadership Coaching: Journeys into the Interior*. Palgrave Macmillan.

Korzybski, A. (2005). *Science and Sanity: An Introduction to Non-Aristotelian Systems and General Semantics* (5th ed., 3rd print). Inst. of General Semantics.

McCall, M. W., Lombardo, M. M., & Morrison, A. M. (1988). *The Lessons of Experience: How Successful Executives Develop on the Job*. Lexington Books.

McClelland, D. C. (2009). *Human Motivation* (Re-issued in digitally printed version). Cambridge University Press.

O'Reilly, C. A., & Pfeffer, J. (2021). Why are grandiose narcissists more effective at organizational politics? Means, motive, and opportunity. *Personality and Individual Differences, 172*, 110557. https://doi.org/10.1016/j.paid.2020.110557

Palsule, S., & Chavez, M. (2020). *Rehumanizing Leadership: Putting Purpose Back into Business*. LID.

Petrie, N. (2014). *Vertical Leadership Development – Part 1: Developing Leaders for a Complex World* (White Paper). Center for Creative Leadership. https://mdvconsulting.co/wp-content/uploads/CCL-VerticalLeadersPart1.pdf

Pink, D. H. (2012). *Drive: The Surprising Truth About What Motivates Us* (Reprint, paperback ed.) Riverhead Books.

Pressfield, S. (2021). *The Legend of Bagger Vance: A Novel of Golf and the Game of Life*. Bantam Books.

Redford, R. (Director). (2000, November 3). *The Legend of Bagger Vance* (Feature Film). DreamWorks.

Roethlisberger, F. J., & Dickson, W. J. (1976). *Management and the Worker: An Account of a Research Program Conducted by the Western Electric Company, Hawthorne Works, Chicago* (17th printing). Harvard University Press.

Rokeach, M. (1973). *The Nature of Human Values*. Free Press.

Roth, S., & Cohen, L. J. (1986). Approach, avoidance, and coping with stress. *American Psychologist, 41*(7), 813–819. https://doi.org/10.1037/0003-066X.41.7.813

Schein, E. H. (1993). *Career Anchors: Discovering Your Real Values* (Rev. ed.) Pfeiffer & Co.

Silver, N. (2020). *The Signal and the Noise: Why so Many Predictions Fail – But Some Don't* (Published with a new preface). Penguin Books.

Smith, C. (2023). *Above Ground: Poems* (First ed.) Little, Brown and Company.

Solnit, R. (2016). *Hope in the Dark: Untold Histories, Wild Possibilities* (Third ed. with a new foreword and afterword). Haymarket Books.

Sonnentag, S., & Fritz, C. (2015). Recovery from job stress: The stressor-detachment model as an integrative framework. *Journal of Organizational Behavior, 36*(S1), S72–S103. https://doi.org/10.1002/job.1924

Stanton, A. (Director). (2012, February). *The clues to a great story* [TED Talk]. https://www.ted.com/talks/andrew_stanton_the_clues_to_a_great_story

Swaminathan, N. (2008, April 29). Why does the brain need so much power? *Scientific American*. https://www.scientificamerican.com/article/why-does-the-brain-need-s/

Tedeschi, R. G. (2020, July). Growth after trauma. *Harvard Business Review*. https://hbr.org/2020/07/growth-after-trauma

Tedeschi, R. G., & Calhoun, L. G. (2004). Posttraumatic growth: Conceptual foundations and empirical evidence. *Psychological Inquiry, 15*(1), 1–18. https://doi.org/10.1207/s15327965pli1501_01

Thomas, R. J. (2008). *Crucibles of Leadership: How to Learn from Experience to Become a Great Leader*. Harvard Business Press.

Transparency to transformation: A chain reaction (CDP Global Supply Chain Report 2020). (2021). https://cdn.cdp.net/cdp-production/cms/reports/documents/000/005/554/original/CDP_SC_Report_2020.pdf?1614160765

Wiseman, L. (2017). *Multipliers: How the Best Leaders Make Everyone Smarter* (Revised and updated edition). Harper Business.

Wu, X., Kaminga, A. C., Dai, W., Deng, J., Wang, Z., Pan, X., & Liu, A. (2019). The prevalence of moderate-to-high posttraumatic growth: A systematic review and meta-analysis. *Journal of Affective Disorders, 243*, 408–415. https://doi.org/10.1016/j.jad.2018.09.023

Index

Pages in *italics* refer to figures and pages followed by "n" refer to notes.

.